HOW FAR
CAN YOU GO?

HOW FAR CAN YOU GO?

MY 25-YEAR QUEST TO WALK AGAIN

JOHN MACLEAN

with Mark Tabb

NEW YORK   BOSTON

Hachette Books
Hachette Book Group
1290 Avenue of the Americas
New York, NY 10104

www.HachetteBookGroup.com

Printed in the United States of America

RRD-C

First edition: March 2016
10 9 8 7 6 5 4 3 2 1

Hachette Books is a division of Hachette Book Group, Inc.

The publisher is not responsible for websites (or their content) that are not owned by the publisher.

The Hachette Speakers Bureau provides a wide range of authors for speaking events. To find out more, go to www.hachettespeakersbureau.com or call (866) 376-6591.

Library of Congress Cataloging-in-Publication Data

Names: Maclean, John, 1966- | Tabb, Mark A.
Title: How far can you go? : my 25-year quest to walk again / John Maclean with Mark Tabb.
Description: First edition. | New York : Hachette Books, [2016]
Identifiers: LCCN 2015044434| ISBN 9780316262859 (hardcover) | ISBN 9781478909323 (audio download) | ISBN 9780316262835 (ebook)
Subjects: LCSH: Maclean, John, 1966- | Athletes—Australia—Biography. | Disabled Persons—Rehabilitation—Australia.
Classification: LCC GV697.M243 A3 2016 | DDC 796.42/57092—dc23
LC record available at http://lccn.loc.gov/2015044434

For my Dad, Alexander Maclean, who loved and encouraged me to try my best and give everything 100%. You said to me, "Look how far you've come, now how far can you go?" What a great question.

Contents

Nothing great is easy.

—*Captain Matthew Webb,*
the first man to swim the English Channel

Preface

I do not believe in coincidences. I do not believe things happen by chance. Everything happens for a reason, even if we do not understand what that reason may be—especially at the time.

I have also found life to be filled with opportunities if we will open our eyes and see the possibilities. And opportunity is just that: a possibility. Life never just hands us anything. As the first man to swim the English Channel—Captain Matthew Webb—famously said, *nothing great is easy*. Given the fact that he uttered these words after swimming more than thirty miles of open ocean in a place where the sea will lie flat one minute then throw twenty-foot swells at you the next, Captain Webb's words are a bit of an understatement. Pursuing possibilities means digging deep within ourselves to find the strength to never give up and never give in, to push through the pain that lasts for a moment to forge the memories that last a lifetime.

Unfortunately, all the hard work and determination in the world do not guarantee success. Sometimes doors slam shut in our faces and no matter how hard we push, they will never open again. However, I have found that every time one door closes, another opens. It's up to us to look for that opening.

This, in a nutshell, is the story of my life. I grew up with big dreams in a working-class family in Australia. I thought all those dreams had been taken from me when I was only twenty-two. But when I stopped feeling sorry for myself and opened my eyes, I found new possibilities awaiting me. The pursuit of those possibilities took me further than even my biggest dreams would have. The question was, *How far could I go?* Little did I know that my pursuits were merely the warm-up act.

In May 2013, I stood up and did something that was, for all intents and purposes, impossible.

Now I am in pursuit of a new set of dreams, again pushing the limits to see how far I can go. Even as I close in on my fiftieth birthday, I believe my story has only begun.

Nothing great is easy. Nor is anything great accomplished alone. Every pursuit requires a team, even the pursuit of goals that appear to be individual accomplishments. In my life, the right people have always come along at just the right time. My closest friendships have been forged in the midst of my greatest challenges. These dear friends have not only pushed me along to reach my goals, but I have pushed them to reach theirs. This isn't just my story; it is theirs as well.

John Maclean
Sydney, New South Wales, Australia

HOW FAR CAN YOU GO?

1

Only Possibilities

I don't remember my mother. I have no memory of her face or her smell or her embrace. Nothing. Everything I know about her came secondhand from my brother Marc or my sister Marion or our father, Alex.

My mother's name was Avril. She married my father when they both lived in a little village just outside of Glasgow, Scotland. My father had been married before. He had three children from his first marriage. A few years after he and my mother married, my father decided to move his new family to the other side of the world and settle just outside of Sydney, Australia. Whatever the reason, he felt he needed a fresh start with his new family, and my mother went along with it. My older brother and sister were both born in Scotland. I came along soon after the move Down Under.

I was still in diapers when my mother's downward spiral began. Before she met my father, she had been diagnosed with and treated for a "severe character disorder of a psychopathic nature." Twice she was admitted into psychiatric hospitals and once she contemplated suicide. My father didn't know any of this when the two of them fell in love. Nor did Avril exhibit any symptoms or show any signs that something might not be quite right. Theirs was a perfectly normal marriage until the stress of a third small child weighed upon her. Unlike when my brother and sister were born, my mother did not have her mother and father to lean on for extra support with me. She was also facing the huge change involved in moving halfway around the world, and she had to deal with that largely alone as my father was away at work, trying to keep the family afloat financially.

I was only ten months old the first time my siblings and I were placed in foster care. My mother had been admitted to the Parramatta Psychiatric Centre and my father had no other option to provide care for us while trying to help my mother heal and hold down his jobs. For my mother, fourteen rounds of electroconvulsive therapy followed, along with numerous medications. Three months later she was home and the family was back together, but it didn't last. A few months after her release a friend found her wandering around an area east of Sydney called the Gap, one of the most beautiful places on earth. But my mother wasn't there for the view. The Gap consists of very high cliffs where Sydney Harbour meets the Pacific Ocean, which makes it a popular suicide spot. She didn't jump, but she told her therapist that she wished she had because she was, in her words, "no good to her husband or children."

Over the next three years my mother was in and out of psychiatric hospitals, while my brother and sister and I went back and forth into foster care. At one point my father sent my mother back to Scotland in the hope that spending time with her family might do her some good. It didn't. Not long after she returned to Australia, she was back at the Gap. Another trip to Parramatta Hospital followed. As soon as she was released she went back to the Gap. She never returned. Her body was found on the rocks below.

I was four. I do not remember any of this. My big brother, Marc, filled me in on all the details years later.

I suppose such childhood trauma should have sent me into the depths of self-pity. But it did not—not then or ever. Feeling sorry for myself, even at a young age, didn't make much sense to me. I reflected on the loss of my mother, later in life, but I knew there was nothing I could have done to save her, nor could I ever bring her back. Instead, when my father remarried a woman named Anne, I was excited to be a family again. A new mom meant my siblings and I left foster care once and for all. From that point forward I dove into my young life with youthful abandon.

Or should I say I ran into life. For me, life always involved running fast and jumping high. Going back to my days in foster care, I found that running faster than anyone else grabbed people's attention, and attention had to be the next best thing to love. When our family got back together after Dad married Anne, the cul-de-sac where we lived turned into a series of never-ending games depending on the season. From touch football to cricket to tennis, all the kids on the street always had some sort of game in play, and I was always in the middle of them. When I had to go off to school, I spent most of my time staring out the window and daydreaming about getting back outside and back into the game.

Beyond the pickup games in the neighborhood, my dad encouraged us as kids to play organized sports because he believed it was a good way to meet friends and burn off excess energy. My speed helped me succeed, and it kept the attention on me. Not only did I beat the other boys in sprints and middle-distance races, I was also asked to try long jumps and high jumps and even racewalking. I did even better with racewalking than running, especially the 1,500 meter. I made it all the way to the state championships in the under-ten-year-old 1,500-meter racewalk, only to be disqualified by a technicality. In racewalking, either your heel or toe must always have contact with the ground. The field marshals watch your feet like a hawk. If both the heel and toe are off the ground at the same time, you receive a warning. Two warnings and you are out. I got two warnings, so I was out of the state champs.

Throughout the next year my coach, Kevin Stone, and I worked on my technique. Again, I made it all the way back to state champs and picked up the bronze medal. The next year I took home the gold. This was very exciting because in the under-12 category in which I now competed, all state champions go on to nationals. The best kids in Little Athletics around the country traveled to Bruce Stadium in Canberra. I remember my brother Marc running on the other side of the oval cheering me on during the race. It felt amazing crossing the finish line in first place as I added a second gold medal to my collection. I'm sure Mom and Dad and my brother Marc and sister Marion were very proud. When I arrived back at school after nationals, the headmaster asked me to join him at an assembly where I was honored in front of the entire school. I liked attention, but not that much attention. The assembly didn't sit very well with me.

As I grew a little older my sports fantasies moved from racing to football. I loved the game. Since my story takes place in Australia, the football I loved is quite different from the American variety played with pads and helmets and the like. We actually have three sports often called football: Australian rules football, rugby union, and rugby league football. All three are similar to American football, complete with hard hits and tackles, except we don't suit up like a gladiator and the action doesn't stop between plays. Rugby league football is the roughest of the three and is generally regarded as the toughest team sport on the planet, so of course, that's what I wanted to play.

All the kids in the neighborhood played football for as far back as I can remember. I started playing organized ball when I was nine and my dad signed me up on my first junior league team. From the moment I first stepped on the field, I knew I'd found my game. I remember once when I was perhaps seven, my father wouldn't let me go out to play football one Saturday because it was raining. I was devastated. A Saturday without football might as well be a school day. I loved the game and I was good at it. For me, life was all about speed, and from the beginning I was faster than most of the guys I played against. I also had a few tricks up my sleeve. In a game when I was about ten, I had the ball, running down the field against one of the top teams in our division. Up ahead a boy lowered his head and got ready to tackle me. As he dove toward me, I jumped and hurdled over him. I didn't stop running until I scored. After the game the referee came over to me. "That was some play you made," he said, "and it's all well and good that you scored, but you need to watch yourself. That's the kind of move that's going to get you hurt." Later I discovered it was his son that I had leapt over.

I kept coming up against this same player. His name was Colin Thomas. It turns out he was always one of the best, if not the best, player on his teams, just like I was on mine. Before long the two of us ended up on the same travel team. His dad came by and picked me up in their family Volkswagen Beetle for the drive down the mountain where we lived to the practice site. Colin and I got to know one another pretty well in those half-hour commutes. Both of us dreamed of playing professional football someday.

After we both graduated from our respective high schools, we started training together to push one another toward our goal of playing the game we loved for actual money. I landed a spot on the under-23 minor league team of our closest professional team, the Penrith Panthers. Technically, that made me a professional athlete, although the salary was so low that the team had to help players land jobs with local businesses to keep us afloat. Thanks to the Panthers, I went to work as an assistant maintenance man at a grade school. On the field I had a great first year with the Panthers. Another season or two like the first, I thought, and I might get to move up to the big league team. Unfortunately, I spent most of my second season sitting on the bench after a falling-out with the coach. At the end of the season I was informed that my services were no longer needed. Rather than give up my dream, I signed on with the Warragamba Wombats, a semipro team.

While I bounced between Penrith and Warragamba, Colin went to work for a fitness and aquatic center. The two of us kept training with each other to keep our football dreams alive. *With* each other isn't exactly the correct term. We really trained *against* one another. Everything we did turned into a no-holds-barred competition. If Colin bench-pressed 200 pounds, I had to do 210, which made him do 220 and me 230 and on and on until neither one of us could lift our hands above our heads. The winner of our competitions always won a fabulous prize, something exotic like a roast chicken or a fresh fruit salad. We once raced on the beach for a seafood dinner. I don't know that I have ever enjoyed a seafood dinner more. That's just how Colin and I were. Maybe it went back to the day we first met on the football field and I hurdled over him when he tried to tackle me. Although we were great friends, we couldn't ride our bikes down the street without it turning into a race.

One day Colin suggested a new competition. "I overheard some of the guys down at the club talking about doing this year's Nepean Triathlon. I think we should enter." At that moment every-thing I knew about triathlons came from watching the Hawaiian Ironman on television in Colin's living room, but I still said, "Sure. Let's give it a go. I will enjoy beating you in something new."

In the weeks leading up to my first Nepean Triathlon, I did a minimal amount of triathlon-specific training. Colin and I raced our bikes up and down the Blue Mountains near our homes. I also ran a little more than usual. It didn't take much to get me to run. I loved running. Sprints. Distance. It didn't matter. Back in 1986 the Nepean's run segment was 12K, or just under seven and a half miles. I felt confident that even if Colin had a big lead on me going into the last segment, I could make up any deficit with my legs. I did not feel the same confidence about the swim. Growing up I never bothered much with swimming. I could do the breaststroke well enough to keep from drowning. I didn't see much point in learning anything new for this one race. I'd never tried doing the breaststroke for a full kilometer, but I figured, how hard could it be?

I soon learned it was extremely hard. My breaststroke turned out to be just a notch or two above a dog paddle. I was one of the last ones out of the water. Colin actually knew how to swim properly. From the start he left me in his wake. He still had a lead after the 40K, or twenty-five-mile, bike segment. But, just as I had predicted, I passed him in the 12K run and never looked back. I never let him hear the end of how easily I beat him.

Of course, Colin being Colin, he wanted a rematch. I had to give it to him. Now that I knew what it took to compete in a triathlon, I started training a little more seriously for the 1987 Nepean. I learned to swim properly, logging many laps in a local pool with one of my mates from the Wombats, John Young. Johnno and I started spending quite a bit of time training together. I also put in more miles on my bike and ran just a little more than the year before. Unfortunately, when I woke up on the morning of the 1987 Nepean Triathlon, I knew this was not going to be my day. I'd come down with a bit of a bug, which not only slowed me down, it also took away my kick at the end. I didn't have enough left in the run segment to catch Colin. He never let me hear the end of it. So, of course, me being me, I told him, "Okay, mate, next year is the decider. We'll see who wins!"

I was still not a serious triathlete, at least not in my mind. I remained a football player with big league dreams. But with so much riding on the 1988 Nepean Triathlon, I started training months ahead of time. I went out and bought a new bike. I paid $800 for a Malvern Star, which was quite a bit of money for a bike back then. This was the finest bike I'd had since my father gave me a racing bike for my fourteenth birthday. Unfortunately, that story didn't exactly have a happy ending. I rode that bike so much on the day my father gave it to me that I was too tired to put it away when I came home for dinner. Instead, I just dropped it on the lawn in front of our house. I planned on going out for another spin after I ate, but I went off to bed instead. The next morning my bike was gone. I never saw it again. I thought a lot about that bike when I bought my new one eight years later. No matter what, I wasn't going to let anything happen to this bike.

Colin and I spent a lot of time up in the Blue Mountains on training rides. Going up the mountains was grueling, but coming back down was worth it. Once or twice I got up over fifty miles per hour. I kept pushing, trying to hit sixty, a mile a minute, but I could never quite get there. "You know," I told Colin one day, "I bet if we had a tandem racing bike, we could do it."

For me, this was more than just a crazy idea. I knew a guy in St. Clair who customized bikes. I gave him a call and he went to work on our super bike. Around the same time, I moved out of my parents' house and moved in with a friend, Mike Winter. Football season had begun and my triathlon training started paying dividends on and off the field. I was having the best year of my life in rugby league. If I kept this up, I knew I would be able to move up a grade and get a little closer to my dream of playing football at the highest level. Just in case this didn't work out, I applied for a position with the local fire department. I was twenty-two years old. Life felt like an open door to boundless possibilities.

On Monday, June 27, 1988, I set off to go visit my friend in St. Clair to see how the tandem bike was coming along. St. Clair was about twenty-five miles away. Rather than drive, I set out on my bike. I was feeling good. The day before, I'd played one of my best football games of the season. I took the day off from my day job at the primary school. The day was too perfect to waste at work. Instead, I put on my headphones, cranked up the Talking Heads, my favorite band at the time, and set out for St. Clair. I took the M4 highway, which is very much like an American four-lane interstate highway, except cars and trucks share the road with bicyclists. Australians are nuts about fitness, which is why bikes are allowed on major highways. I always stayed on the shoulder, which was wide enough that I never felt unsafe on the road.

Most of the trip to St. Clair was downhill. At one point I managed to hit fifty miles per hour. I pushed as hard as I could to move the needle higher, but I could not. *The tandem will do it*, I told myself. That only made me more anxious to see the bike finished and try it out. My stay in St. Clair was brief. I wanted to get back on the road while my muscles were still loose. A long, hard climb lay ahead of me. In a sick way I looked forward to it, not to the pain such a steep incline demanded, but to the challenge of it. The push up the mountain would leave my legs and chest burning, but nothing would feel better than getting to the top.

I headed back onto the M4 and started toward the big hill ahead of me. Standing on the pedals, I lowered my head and pedaled hard to build a good cadence while avoiding the broken bottles and other trash that pile up on highway shoulders. Traffic buzzed past me. I looked up. I still had a bit to go before I attacked the hill. I took a deep breath and pushed harder to build momentum before I hit the incline. That is my last memory of my ride.

A truck driver coming up behind me at just under seventy miles per hour glanced over his shoulder to see if the lane was clear to pass another vehicle. As he glanced over his shoulder, the eight-ton box truck filled with empty fire extinguishers drifted slightly onto the shoulder. The lane was clear. The driver accelerated and changed lanes. If he had listened closely, he might have heard the sound of one of his headlights shattering along with the lens of the turn signal. But he didn't. Nor did he feel the slight nudge of the truck rumbling over something on the road. He didn't notice anything out of the ordinary until a motorcycle came racing up to him nearly a mile down the road. The motorcyclist frantically motioned for him to pull over, which he did. The truck driver wondered if the motorcyclist had lost his mind.

Thirteen-year-old Michael McKenzie sat in the backseat of his mother's car as she headed east toward Sydney. Bored, he stared idly out the window, watching the traffic in the opposite lanes zip by. "What? Stop!" he screamed at his mother as he saw a body and a silver bicycle flipping end over end up into the air on the other side of the highway. A truck briefly obscured his view. When it passed, he saw the body bounce along the ground and come to rest wedged up against the guardrail. His mother pulled over. Before she could ask him what was wrong, he flew out of the car, darted across the median, and ran to the broken man lying on the pavement. Another car had stopped. A priest was already next to the body, administering last rites.

A police car from nearby Penrith arrived next. A call had come in that a bicyclist had been struck and killed on the M4. Such calls are, unfortunately, not uncommon. An ambulance had also been dispatched. When it arrived, paramedics found a crumpled body lying under the guardrail that leads to the Kingswood Road over-pass. A bowed silver bike lay off to one side. To their surprise, I was still breathing. They loaded me into the ambulance, but they doubted I would survive the twenty-five-mile drive to Sydney's Westmead Hospital emergency room.

2

Back from the Brink

My father tells me my first words in the hospital were, "How's my bike?" I don't remember saying that, but it sounds like me. I loved that bike. My father held on to my words as a reason to hope I would pull through. When he first arrived at the hospital, he was told to prepare himself for the worst. I was not expected to live.

I do not remember the accident or my first few days in the hospital. My first memory is waking up in the intensive-care unit, struggling to breathe. My face hurt and I could not understand why. My mind cleared enough to realize I had an oxygen mask over my nose and mouth. The pain from the mask's pressure on my nose made me wince. Slowly I became aware of the rest of my body. My skin felt like someone had taken a grinder to me from head to toe. I lifted my arm. Wires and tubes connected it to beeping machines around me. The more awake I became, the more I hurt. Pain shot at me from every corner of my body. Every corner except my legs, that is. I couldn't feel them. From the prone position in which I was lying, I couldn't see them either. Panicked, I pressed the nurse call button with my left thumb over and over like a deranged contestant on *Jeopardy!* After what felt like an eternity but was in truth perhaps thirty seconds, a nurse came into my room.

"Where are my legs?" I asked as she entered the room. "What happened to my legs? Have they been amputated?"

"No, no, John; they're right here," she said. She pulled the sheet back and lifted them, one at a time, for me to see.

I was so relieved I passed out.

I spent most of that week moving in and out of consciousness. My injuries were massive, or exactly what one might expect after being run over by an eight-ton truck. I suffered a pulmonary contusion, retroperitoneal hemorrhage, head trauma, chest trauma, vertebral trauma, and pelvic trauma. I broke my back in three places, my pelvis in four, and my right arm in two places. I also had a broken sternum and scrapes and abrasions from the pavement. When I first arrived at the trauma center, they pumped seven units of blood into me. The ER doctors shared the paramedics' doubts about my ability to survive. One of the male nurses in the room later told me that during the frantic attempts to save my life, one of the doctors actually referred to my condition as "mahogany or pine?"—as in the type of coffin that would be selected. They believed I would not survive.

I have a hazy recollection that I could have chosen to give up and die. Death's door beckoned me. All I needed to do was open it and the indescribable pain would be over. Yet I clearly recall saying to myself, "I don't want to *die*! I *don't* want to die!"

Close friends and family surrounded me. My dad and mom, brother Marc, and sister Marion stayed close by. My girlfriend at the time was there as well. Colin came to see me. The sight of my broken body in the hospital bed was more than he could take. His knees grew weak; his stomach lurched. He tried to move away from me but he only got as far as the bedside curtain before throwing up. The charge nurse made him clean it up himself. Also my teammate from Warragamba John Young, who lived over an hour away from the hospital, came to see me every week, without fail, for four months.

Once I was stable enough for transport, I was airlifted from Westmead to the Royal North Shore Hospital, one of two Sydney hospitals with a spinal unit. I vaguely remember the thumping of the helicopter blades. As injured as I was, I also recall being excited about riding in a helicopter for the first time. Perhaps that tells you everything you need to know about my personality. My family had cause to be optimistic with the move. In the top right-hand corner of my discharge papers was the notation, "Discharged to survive." I was officially off the critical list. I was not, however, out of the ICU.

After a few more days in the ICU at Royal North Shore, they placed me in the acute care spinal unit. For the next eight weeks I lay on my back, staring up at the ceiling and counting the bricks outside my window. The morphine they gave me kept me in a fog. When my brain cleared enough to comprehend where I was and why I was there, I nearly drowned in fear. The pain was so intense. Lying in bed, it felt like someone had crept under me with a blowtorch with which they were now torturing me. The hospital tried several different beds, looking for a way to relieve my pain. Nothing worked. When the pain grew so excruciating that I could not bear it, I received more pain meds that immediately put me back into the deep fog. Depression set in. I understood why spinal patients are closely monitored. Many find it easier to end it all rather than deal with the pain and the loss of use of one's limbs. I was one of the lucky ones. Only my legs seemed to be affected.

At some point during my eight weeks on my back, Colin came back to see me. He brought along my friend Warren Hurst. The two of them rode their bikes nearly thirty miles into Sydney to visit me, even braving the heavy traffic of the Sydney Harbour

Bridge. On their way into my room, a nurse handed them a fruit salad she'd just made for me out of all the fruit well-wishers had sent. The nurse intended for them to give it to me. Colin and Warren had other ideas. Without saying a word, the two walked in and proceeded to eat the entire salad in front of me. When they finished the last bits of fruit, they turned around, dropped their bike pants, and mooned me. After pulling their pants back up, Colin turned and said, "We gotta get back." They rode their bikes thirty miles and spoke only these four words. Then they walked out the door.

Lying there, helpless to do anything, I couldn't force any words out. I wasn't angry. Well, I was over the salad, but I wasn't angry with Colin. This prank was his way of saying, "I got you this time. Now get up out of that bed and try to get me back."

Getting up out of the bed was easier said than done. Oddly enough, no one ever came in and had "the talk" with me. No one, not a doctor or my father or my brothers or sister, ever looked me in the eye and said, "John, you will probably never walk again." At least I don't remember such a talk, and believe me—I would remember *that*. Running was my life. I don't think I could forget someone informing me that that life was now gone.

Perhaps no one told me because it should have been obvious to me. I learned that one of the three breaks in my back injured my spine at the twelfth thoracic vertebra (T12). However, my spinal cord was not completely severed. A small sliver remained. Officially that makes me an incomplete paraplegic. After all my other injuries healed and I was able to start physical therapy, I found I had perhaps 25 percent use of my left leg, while my right hardly worked at all. That was the good news and I seized on it. From the start I was determined to get my old life back. The doctors told me that the first two years after my accident were critical. "Wherever you are in terms of your motor skills after two years is likely where you will be the rest of your life," they said repeatedly. To me, that meant I had two years to get back on my feet and not only walk but run again. I still harbored dreams of playing professional football and taking advantage of all the possibilities that lay before me when I pulled my bike out onto the M4 that sunny June day.

I was never told getting my old life back was impossible, perhaps because no one, not my neurologist or any of the team of therapists with which I worked, knew how much progress I might make. Every spinal cord injury is different, as is every patient's recovery. Looking back, I am sure they had a pretty good idea of how far I would go. However, no one ever came in and burst my dreams of walking and running again. My family encouraged me to keep pushing. My brother Marc told me over and over, "John, you need to think of your recovery as a race. This will be a marathon, not a sprint. But you'll get to the finish line. Don't worry." Marc is a nurse, so I seized on to his words as more than just the encouragement of one brother to another.

I also grabbed ahold of the words of my family doctor. Dr. Atif Gabreal had been patching me back together since I was a kid. Pretty early on into my recovery he came to see me in the hospital. "Don't worry, John," he told me with that deep, authoritative doctor voice. "One day you will be bigger, stronger, and faster than ever before." If anyone should know, I reasoned, it was Dr. Gabreal. I did not stop and consider the fact that he was not part of the medical team caring for me, nor had he examined my charts in any detail. He was simply there as a friend, and friends give one another hope. Years later Dr. Gabreal told me he was so devastated by the sight of me broken in that hospital bed that he had to say something to encourage me.

During my first couple of months in the hospital words were

about the only thing I had to hold on to. I had to lie still in bed and not move. The one day I defied that order and used all of my strength to roll over on my own I received a stern rebuke from the charge nurse. I felt like a little boy. In a way I was. I had no control over anything happening to me, while every shred of dignity I had was stripped away. A catheter drained my bladder, while daily enemas took care of the rest of my waste system. Several times a day orderlies came in and flipped me over in my bed. Each time they did, bits of broken skin and scabs stuck to the bedding and ruptured as they lifted me up, causing new levels of pain to shoot through my body. I endured regular sponge baths, which I hated. There's nothing pleasant about a rough sponge being dragged across broken flesh. I didn't even have a say about my hair. A hospital barber came in and cut it whenever the staff deemed necessary.

My first step toward regaining my old life—a life I controlled, not some hospital staffer—came when my nurse mentioned that they planned on gradually weaning me off the morphine that kept my pain manageable. "Gradually?" I said. "I don't think so," I thought. "I'm a football player and I can take a hit." Cut it off cold turkey.

The nurse looked at me like I was a little touched in the head. "If that's what you want," he said.

"That's what I want," I replied. My reason was simple. I'd been on the drugs long enough. I didn't want to risk adding addiction to the long list of obstacles I had to overcome to get back to my old life.

Finally the day came when my spinal specialist, Dr. John Yeo, told me I was cleared to do more than lie still. "That's what I have been waiting to hear," I said. Dr. Yeo just smiled. Throughout my time in the hospital he became a good friend and mentor. We remain close to this day.

With Dr. Yeo's blessing, I threw myself into my rehab. Just sitting up proved to be a challenge, but I kept at it like I had once run into opposing lines on the football field. I planned on winning this fight. I announced to the hospital psychologist, Helen, that I would walk out the hospital doors when I was released. The first order of business, however, was to regain full use of my right hand. The accident had badly damaged the radial nerve. Thankfully the nerve regenerated and I regained full use of my hand after long sessions of occupational therapy. I saw regaining use of my hand as a sign that my legs were next.

Much of my physical therapy took place in the hydrotherapy pool. I loved the sense of freedom the water gave me. Decked out in a makeshift flotation device, I almost felt normal in the water. I couldn't swim laps at first, but eventually I managed to swim the twenty-five-meter length of the pool. Looking back, that twenty-five-meter swim is perhaps my biggest achievement in the water.

The staff at Royal North Shore Hospital were amazing. I think the longer I was there the more I appreciated each and every one of them. They were hard taskmasters, but they were doing their best to assist everyone in the best way they could. I remember the physical therapist named Debbie. I was on the gymnastic mats in my tracksuit pants, and she told me to get on my knees and try to crawl. I guess the old saying holds true—you have to crawl before you can walk. I got down on my hands and knees when suddenly Debbie pushed me, not hard, just a gentle nudge, but that was enough to topple me over. I struggled to get back into a crawling position when she pushed me over again. I thought, *Why is Debbie pushing me over?* Before I could ask her she explained that she was evaluating what muscles I had control over and which ones I did not. That made me feel a little better, until I thought a little more about what was happening. I used to play football against a bunch of guys much bigger than Debbie. *If she can push me over this easily, I still have a long way to go.*

A few weeks into my rehab, out of the blue, I happened upon a reminder of my old life. Back when I played for the Penrith Panthers under-23 team, our biggest fan was a young woman named Rhonda. Rhonda was at every game, waving her Panthers flag, cheering like crazy. Before my accident, she was the only person I'd ever met who was confined to a wheelchair. After one of our games, the team held an event in the club across the street from the stadium. (Keep in mind this is Australian rugby league football. The team doesn't just play in the city. There's a team "club" that any of our fans can join. Membership grants access to the club, which is a complex with multiple restaurants, grand halls, and even a casino.) I ran into Rhonda. She asked me to have a dance with her. Now, I wasn't too good at dancing with anyone, let alone someone in a wheelchair, but I said, "Of course." I moved about with the music the best I could, and the two of us had a nice little dance.

I had not seen Rhonda since the Panthers told me my services were no longer needed, until I ran into her in the spinal unit. She was there for some sort of procedure for her back. Just seeing her brought back a flood of memories of my time with the Panthers. She snapped me out of my déjà vu when she said, "I'm sorry about your accident, John."

"Thanks, Rhonda," I said. There wasn't much more to the conversation than that, just a bit of small talk, but it made me flash back to our brief dance. Let me tell you, I was very happy I did not let my uneasiness with dancing keep me from giving her that moment. Thinking about that night also reminded me of the man I once was. Although a short time on the calendar had passed since then, it now felt like another life completely. Thinking back to who I once was only made me that much more determined to beat these injuries and get back on the dance floor on my own two feet.

My first real, honest look of where I was came on what should have been a triumphant day. I had finally progressed far enough that I could move out of my wheelchair and onto a toilet by myself. Just that simple act placed me far ahead of many of my fellow spinal unit patients who never regain control of their bladder and bowels. I made the big move and was feeling pretty good about myself until I caught a glimpse of myself in the bathroom mirror. I did not recognize the ashen, emaciated figure staring back at me. Both my arm and leg muscles had shriveled to nothing. My normally sun-bleached hair had turned dark. Scars covered my face and body. I looked closer. The dull eyes staring back at me were sunk back into my skull. Now I understood the looks on the faces of everyone who came to visit me.

I could not stand the sight of this stranger. He actually scared me. The thought that this could be me forever sent chills down my spine, at least to the T12. Who would ever be interested in me? Would I ever have a wife? Family? What is life going to look like? Once the initial horror wore off, I became more determined than ever that this would not be the end of my story.

These legs would work again.

I would get up out of this wheelchair.

I would regain my old life.

I had passion. I had determination. I was willing to do whatever it took to make my goal a reality.

If only life were so simple.

3

Starting Over

Four months after my accident I "walked" out of the hospital. It was not, however, the triumphant victory lap I had envisioned. In my mind, I planned to walk out on my own two feet without assistance from anyone or anything. That's not quite what happened. I wheeled myself into the elevator, where I leaned heavily upon a pair of forearm crutches and pushed myself up from my chair and onto my wobbly legs. When the elevator doors opened to the hospital lobby, I lurched forward on the crutches, my weight supported by my arms. My left leg helped me keep my balance while my right leg, tucked in behind, came along for the ride. I hobbled across the lobby, past the admissions desk, and out the front door. Once outside, I negotiated a slight rise up the sidewalk to where the car was parked. My dad pushed my chair next to me and I collapsed into it, exhausted and hurting.

Even though my "walk" didn't quite measure up to what I had imagined, the fact that I left the hospital upright on my feet gave me a great deal of hope. To me, these were the first steps toward turning back the clock and reclaiming my old life. Only four months had passed since the truck ran over me on the highway.

If I can walk with crutches already, just think where I will be a couple of years from now, I told myself.

Getting my old life back was not the only thing driving me. I hated life in a wheelchair. I hated the way people looked at me in it. I hated being shorter than everyone else. I hated having to rely on other people to do things for me that I couldn't do for myself in that dreaded chair. Truth be told, I wanted nothing to do with it. The sooner I could be out of it and on my feet, the happier I would be.

Those who have never lived in a wheelchair have no idea what it is like to suddenly go from being a healthy, strong athlete to a shell of your former self, wheeling about. People stared at me wherever I went. I knew what they had to think of me. I thought it myself. I could see their looks of pity. I could hear their minds ticking off that inevitable, unspoken question on the tips of their tongues: *I wonder what happened to you?* People do it without thinking. It's a reflex reaction. A young, otherwise healthy young man in a wheelchair equals a tragedy. I don't know what was worse: the quizzical, double-take stares or the sad faces brimming with sympathy and concern.

I also hated the new label affixed to me as if it had been tattooed in the middle of my forehead. Officially, I was now disabled. *Disabled.* Everything about the word repulses me. When you "dis" someone, you speak disrespectfully or critically of them. "Dis" expresses negation, a reversal or absence of an action or state. According to society, all of that and more was now me. I was permanently dissed. The very idea makes me cringe. To be disabled is society's way of saying quite clearly, "You are less than others. Move aside." Where I had always approached life with no limits, only possibilities, I found myself labeled as one with nothing but limitations. I had always prided myself on my speed and agility on the football field and my overall devotion to health and fitness. Many *disabled* people dream of such things.

My wheelchair embodied "disabled." The only way out from under the label, I believed, was to regain the use of my legs and tell the chair good-bye forever. So that is what I set out to do. Every morning for two years my dad drove me to a hydrotherapy pool near our home where I did lap after lap. From there it was off to a local gym owned by a friend from my days with the Penrith Panthers, Ron Oaxley. Ron worked as a trainer for the team. After a hard workout at Ron's gym, it was back to the house for lunch and a nap. More workouts followed in the afternoon. My friend John Young helped put together a makeshift gym in my garage. Johnno welded specialized equipment for me and even wrote my training programs. Most afternoons he came over after work, and the two of us pushed each other the way Colin and I used to.

The training worked, but not in the way I had hoped. Progress with my legs came slowly if at all. I tried to ignore this fact by working my upper body even harder. I soon regained the body mass four months in the hospital had taken away from me. My increased upper body strength made it easier for me to navigate about on my forearm crutches. I say it made it easier, but moving about with the crutches was still not easy. Day after day I strapped them to my forearms and set out trying to walk. I cannot count the number of laps I did up and down our street, sweat pouring off of me from the effort. My legs still didn't work any better than the day I left the hospital. The left leg supported a little of my weight while the right still dragged behind as I hobbled along on those crutches. Still, I forced myself to use them as much as possible rather than give in to the chair.

One particular morning I hobbled into Ron's gym on my crutches. Ron grinned at my progress. "Johnny Mac, I never want to see you in that chair again," he said. He was trying to encourage me to keep pushing and not let the accident beat me.

"That's my plan, Ron," I replied.

However, with each passing day it became more and more clear to me that my plan wasn't working. It wasn't just the lack of progress with my legs that discouraged me. Working so hard to get my old life back left me exhausted. Of the first three years after my accident, I probably slept through two of them. Early every evening I stumbled off to bed and slept at least twelve hours every night. Even that wasn't enough sleep. I napped another two to four hours every single afternoon. I had no choice. My body simply shut down and told me it was going to sleep and I was cordially invited to join it. Life was going on around me while I slept through it.

If I could see progress toward my goal of walking and running again, the exhaustion would be worth it, but in truth, I wasn't making any. In spite of all the hours and effort I was putting into turning back the clock, I still could not walk in any functional way. I tried to convince myself otherwise. With each hobbling journey on my crutches I told myself I was that much closer to walking, but I knew I was only fooling myself. Not only did my legs not work, but my efforts to walk caused excruciating pain thanks to the hypersensitivity that little sliver of spinal cord gave me. Life felt like a cruel joke. It was as if the small part of my spinal cord still intact was programmed to only carry signals of pain up from my legs while completely ignoring my brain's commands telling my legs to move.

One afternoon after pushing myself through my workouts, I went back to my room, frustrated and angry. For the first time since I started my rehab, I got very honest with myself. Tears welled up in my eyes, but I fought them back. Then my dad came into my room. One look at him and I could no longer hold back the emotions building inside me. "I'm trying as hard as I can, but nothing is happening," I said. Dad looked at me as only a parent can, and I got the sense he already knew what I could not admit to myself: I was never going to walk again. I finally realized that no matter how hard you try, paraplegia is not something you beat. Dad looked at me and I cried big, heartfelt tears. Dad was misty eyed too, although he held it together. I gave him a hug and just wept.

Finally Dad said, "Look how far you've come," referring to my surviving the accident and even having the possibility of something approaching a normal life, albeit in a wheelchair. "Now," he added, "how far can you go?"

Something about my father's words resonated deep inside of me. For more than two years all I wanted to do was turn back the clock. Every day I looked back at what I had once been and I told myself I had to find a way to get back there. Failure was not an option. Sitting in my room with my dad, I finally admitted to myself the truth I could not outrun. A truck had hit me, breaking my back in three places. My spine had been partially severed and I was now a paraplegic. For two years I clung to the "incomplete" in my diagnosis, as if I could push myself from incomplete paraplegic to fully healed. I couldn't, no matter how hard I tried.

When I finally accepted the reality of my situation, I felt as if the weight of my old life was lifted from my shoulders. For the first time since I pedaled out onto the M4, I could honestly, expectantly ask what the future may hold. I could never look ahead as long as I clung to the past. Once I freed myself of the past, the future looked bright and promising. Since I was a little boy I had dreamed of being a professional athlete. I was still young, and honestly, with the exception of my legs, I was probably in the best shape of my life. *How far can I go?* I wondered. *If I stop looking down on myself in my chair, what might I be able to accomplish?*

Even before this conversation with my father, I had started to explore other outlets for my athletic and competitive drive. Johnno and I bought a two-man kayak together. The first couple of times we tried using it we ended up flipped upside down in the water. Once we learned how to sit in it without toppling it over, we started paddling the Nepean River together. One afternoon the two of us set out on the river after Johnno got off work. We planned on doing a long paddle, pushing ourselves to see how far we could go. However, the sun went down earlier than we expected, and we missed our turnaround mark in the river. I thought we had gone too far when I asked Johnno if he thought we ought to turn back. "No, I think it is just around the next bend," he said. The next bend turned into another and another and another until the two of us were lost on the river in the dark. By the time we finally found our way back to where we'd parked the car, we'd paddled more than twenty miles. That episode told me something, besides reminding me that when in doubt on the river, turn around. Paddling twenty miles in the dark told me not being able to use my legs had not changed me. I could still go farther and faster.

Johnno and I kept training together and paddling together. In 1990 we entered the Hawkesbury Classic two-person kayak race, better known as Madness by Moonlight. Covering nearly seventy miles from Windsor to Brooklyn by river, the race started at 5:00 p.m. Johnno and I crossed the finish line at a little after five the next morning. We placed twelfth out of one hundred. I was disappointed with our finish (I had my sights set on gold, as I always do no matter what I am doing), but we did well enough to keep my athletic dreams alive. A couple of years later we won the New South Wales two-man kayak state championships. I will never forget the looks on the faces of some of our competitors when I got out of the kayak and climbed into my wheelchair.

Success in the kayak reassured me that I was on the right track. Then I came across something that opened up a whole new world to me. Although I loved running, I also loved the sense of speed and freedom that came from riding my bike. Since you can't ride a bike without legs, that love was no longer available to me—that is, until the day in early 1994 when I came across a handcycle that had been imported from the United States. A handcycle is a three-wheeled bike with a seat that sits low and a pair of hand pedals that sit at chest level. The pedals move in unison with one another, unlike a standard bike, where the pedals are offset 180 degrees. Compared to handcycles today, this model was a beast of a machine, weighing in at more than thirty-seven pounds, but to me, it meant freedom. I even dubbed it the Freedom Rider. As soon as I climbed on it, a lightbulb went off. I knew what I *had* to do next. I went to Johnno and said to him, "I need to finish what I started. I'm going to do the Nepean Triathlon."

"Okay, mate; let's give it a go," Johnno said. Unlike me, he'd never done a triathlon, but such a trivial detail never stopped Johnno.

I knew I could handle the one-kilometer swim portion of the race. I had long since graduated from swimming laps in the hydrotherapy pool to swimming distances in the local Penrith Lakes. The lakes had originally been made out of old quarries. After it was announced that Sydney was to host the 2000 Olympics, the lakes were expanded and transformed into a world-class rowing and regatta center. The lakes were my favorite place to swim, and they were close to my house.

I also felt confident I could handle the 12K "run." I did not have a racing chair, nor had it ever entered my mind to get one. All I had was my regular day chair, but I knew it was enough. Four years after I made peace with my chair, wheeling twelve kilometers felt

as intimidating as running that distance had before my accident—
that is, not at all.

The handcycle, however, was something new. I got the hang
of it easily enough. Cranking the two pedals with my arms in a
"push-pull" motion works a different muscle set than the downward motion on the push rims of the wheels of my chair, although
both tax my arms and upper body. If I hoped to pedal twenty-five
miles, I needed to do some serious road training. And there was
only one place I knew that had the long, straight stretches of road
I needed: the M4.

I have to tell you, the first time Johnno and I cycled out onto
the M4, my heart was beating in my ears. This wasn't my first time
on the M4. Because it is the primary highway between my then
home in Penrith and Sydney, I drove up and down it at least once
a week for six years before Johnno and I rode our bikes down it.
Every trip I had to pass the place where the truck hit me. However,
there is a huge difference between motoring past that spot in the
safety of an automobile and being back out on the pavement on a
bike, especially a handcycle.

A funny thing happened on my first training ride down the
M4. Johnno and I came upon the exact spot where the accident
occurred, but I didn't stop and look around. Instead I kept going.
I'm still here. I didn't die. I'm moving on, I told myself as I rode
past. Part of my life was frozen in that small stretch of asphalt, but
with every crank of the pedals I felt the past lose a little more of its
hold on me. Yes, the accident was a turning point in my life, but
my life did not end there in any way, shape, or form. I changed,
certainly, but now it was up to me to decide what I would do with
that change. Riding down the M4 training for the very event for
which I was training on the day the truck hit me was my way of
saying I had decided to go forward.

My bold confidence started to give way as the day of the actual Nepean Triathlon approached. I felt certain I could finish the race. I never doubted that for a moment. However, my mind flashed back to the day I climbed out of the kayak after winning the New South Wales championships and saw the looks on the other competitors' faces. I did not want to go through that again. I remained very self-conscious of the sideways glances and double takes my wheeling up to the start line would elicit. So I came up with a plan. I went to Johnno and asked him to go with me to the course the day before the race when no one else was around. "You can help me in and out of the water and up onto my handcycle, and we will do the course together without me drawing attention to myself with my chair," I said to him. I thought it the perfect solution.

Johnno gave me one of his looks. "What are you talking about?" he said. "You're doing the race with me and everyone else, and that's all there is to it."

"But..." I said.

"But what?" Johnno replied. I knew the conversation was over.

The day of the race, my worst fears were confirmed. People stared. Cameras flashed. I was a bit of a sideshow. Johnno carried me into the water, which elicited more stares and funny looks. But once the starter blew his whistle and I started the swim, all of the prerace awkwardness just sort of evaporated away. In the water I was just another head topped with a green swim cap in a churning sea of green swim caps. At the end of the swim leg, Johnno had to carry me out of the water and help position me onto my handcycle. As soon as he did, I was off and on my own. The rest of the race is a blur, except for the ambulance that trailed me throughout the "run." Multiple times the driver called out, "Are you okay? Do you need help?"

"I'm fine, mate. Thanks," I called back. I struggled a bit with the steepest hill, but once I made it over it, I knew I was going to finish.

The crowd had thinned by the time I crossed the finish line, which was a bit of a relief to me. I still felt self-conscious about my condition. The fewer eyes on me, the better. When I did cross the finish line, a wave of emotion swept over me, a feeling that I had just stepped into a beginning rather than across an end. Not only had I closed the circle going back to the 1988 Nepean, but a new door had opened to me. I no longer felt the need to go back. Instead, I was anxious to go out and see what else I could do. I could still hear my father's words ringing in my ears. "How far can you go?" he asked. I couldn't wait to find out.

4

More than Able

When I did my first two triathlons in 1986 and 1987, I did not foresee any long-term role for triathlons in my life. I was a football player. Besides giving me a new arena to compete against my friend Colin, the sport basically served as nothing more than cross-training to make me stronger and faster for the football field. Then came my trip down the M4 that took away my dreams of playing football for a living. However, the competitive drive in me was still as strong as ever, as were my dreams of competing on the biggest stages available. I couldn't move up to play big league football, but, I wondered after becoming the first wheelie to complete the Nepean Triathlon, would it be possible for me to complete a longer triathlon? I had to find out.

Johnno and I entered the Sri Chinmoy Triathlon in Canberra, which is about 180 miles southwest of Sydney. I didn't have to talk him into it. As best mates, not only did we push one another in our training, but he was always up for any challenge. And the Sri Chinmoy looked like a big one. Each leg was exactly double the length of the Nepean, with a 2K—or just over a mile—swim, a fifty-mile bike leg, and a fifteen-mile run. I borrowed an actual racing chair for this race. A racing chair has three wheels, like a tricycle. The front wheel is smaller and far forward, which allows for much greater downward pressure to be applied to the push rim attached to the main larger wheels. As a result, you can gain much more speed. With the racing chair I felt better about the "run" component. Unfortunately, once the race started I found myself struggling with the bike leg. For the first few miles I felt like the handcycle was fighting me. In a way it was. I discovered the brake had not fully disengaged. Once I released the brakes, I was off like a flash. I finished the Sri Chinmoy, which made me start thinking about the ultimate in triathlon competition: the Ironman.

An Ironman triathlon is the ultimate endurance race, combining a 2.4-mile swim with a 112-mile bike ride followed by a full-marathon, 26.2-mile run. The sport originated on the island of Oahu in Hawaii in 1978 when three friends got into an argument over which of their three favorite long-distance races was the greatest challenge. US naval commander John Collins ended the argument by suggesting they combine the three and do them all in one day. As Collins put it, "Swim 2.4 miles, bike 112 miles, run 26.2 miles, then brag for the rest of your life!" For me, completing an Ironman wasn't so much about bragging for the rest of my life as it was finally proving myself to me. Even after winning kayak races with Johnno and completing two shorter triathlons, I still struggled with accepting myself for who I was, chair and all. If I became an Ironman, I would prove myself the equal of anyone.

When I contacted the director of an Australian Ironman, I discovered I still had a long way to go. The race director turned me down cold when I asked about entering. I pressed, but he shot me down again. "Part of the course includes a narrow footpath on a bridge," he said. "Your chair would keep other competitors from getting through." I offered suggestions of how to keep that from happening, but he wouldn't hear of it. By the time I hung up the phone it was clear to me that he simply did not want a wheelie in his race.

Not long after, I went to visit my sister Marion. We sat in her living room, talking and watching television when *Wide World of Sports* came on. This particular episode featured coverage of the 1994 Ironman World Championship in Kona, Hawaii. The Kona race is the annual running of the original Ironman from 1978. The first race had fifteen competitors. The 1994 race had some fifteen hundred. But that wasn't what grabbed my attention. Part of the television coverage focused on Jon Franks, who was attempting to become the first wheelchair athlete to finish all three legs within the allotted cut-off times for each. The entire race must be completed in seventeen hours, but to go the distance you must complete the 2.4-mile swim in two hours, twenty minutes; the 112-mile bike ride in ten hours, thirty minutes from the start of the race; then wrap it all up in under seventeen hours. Needless to say, I was glued to the television from the moment I saw Franks. Then, when he failed to finish the bike leg in the allotted time and declined the race director's invitation to go ahead and attempt the marathon, I knew a door had just opened. "I'll do it," I told Marion.

"Do what?" she asked.

"Kona. Next year I will be the first wheelie to finish the Hawaiian Ironman."

"I don't doubt you will," Marion replied. Everyone I told about my goal had the same reaction. Whether they believed I could do it or not wasn't nearly as important as whether or not I believed it, and I did. I knew I could do it.

In spite of my bold talk, I needed a little reassurance that I wasn't just fooling myself into believing what I wanted to believe. I read that Jon Franks had completed the Surfers Paradise International Triathlon in Gold Coast, Queensland, Australia. If Franks did it, then that's where I had to go next. In my first two triathlons I had only raced against myself. As the first wheelie to do each race, I had no other times to which to compare myself. The Surfers Paradise gave me a chance to see how I measured up to an elite wheelchair triathlete. After finishing this race that was half the length of the Ironman in seven hours, or exactly forty-five minutes faster than Franks had the year before, I knew I could tackle Kona. Now all I had to do was qualify.

Unlike able-bodied competitors who can qualify for the Kona world championship at any number of events around the world, wheelchair triathletes have one shot each year to punch their ticket. In 1995 that shot came in a half-Ironman triathlon in Panama City, Florida. There, for the first time, I would go head-to-head against Jon Franks. The winner went to Kona; the loser had to sit at home and watch it on television. Johnno could not take time off work to travel with me to Florida. Instead, another good mate, David Wells, went with me. Just as Johnno had done before, David carried me out of the water after the swim leg. When he picked me up, I led the entire field, including all the able-bodied competitors. My moment of elation of being the first one out of the water took a bit of a dive when David tripped running up the beach toward the bike area, sending both of us sprawling across the sand. I have long since learned that life's lessons in humility are always a good thing.

I was not surprised when I beat Franks to qualify for Kona. I was, however, very surprised by a phone call the night before the race. Don, my oldest brother from my father's first marriage, rang me up to wish me luck and to make me a promise. Because Don, along with his sister Morag and brother Kenny, had all been left behind in Scotland when my father and mother moved to Australia before I was born, I had no relationship with any of them growing up. They all later moved to Canada. Prior to his phone call I had only met Don once, and that was when I was sixteen. He had come to Australia for a quick visit, and the two of us spent perhaps an hour together. Now he was on the phone saying, "Dad told me what you are trying to do, and I want to tell you I'm touched. If you qualify, I'll be there with you in Hawaii."

I was stunned. "Are you serious, Don?" I asked. "Would you honestly come all the way to Hawaii?"

"Just qualify and I'll be there," he replied.

That wasn't Don's only surprise for me. When I called him after the race and said, "We're going to Hawaii," he replied, "Let me see what I can do for you." Don worked for Canadian Airlines, which flew out of Sydney. He spoke with the airline and arranged for them to cover my race-related travel, even flying me back to Florida, where I trained in the month leading up to the 1995 Hawaiian Ironman. Looking back, I can honestly say that connecting with my brother was the greatest thing to come out of my qualifying for my first Ironman. I later flew to Canada, where I got to know Morag and Kenny as well.

For most people, Hawaii equals paradise. Those people have never attempted the Ironman Triathlon in Kona.

The race begins pleasant enough. Johnno and David Wells carried me out into the water, where I waited with my 1,500 fellow competitors from all over the world and all walks of life for the cannon to fire to start the race. I was the only one in a wet suit, a concession race officials made to give me added buoyancy due to my inability to use my legs. Very few people knew about this arrangement, which caused one of the other racers to yell over with an angry tone, "Hey, why are *you* in a wet suit?"

Before I could say a word, a fellow Australian, Gordon Bell, answered, "He's in a wheelchair, you idiot."

That was the last complaint I heard regarding my wet suit, and the last disparaging word I heard from another competitor. As I waited in the water, surrounded by all these people with the same dream of becoming an Ironman, I tried to take in the entire scene and grab hold of the memory. The morning sun burned off the thin blanket of mist that hung on the water. Helicopters buzzed overhead while athletes shuffled and stamped in the water, loosening their muscles. A few conversations went on around me, but I didn't really notice what anyone said. Their voices mixed into the sounds coming at me. I glanced around and gave myself a moment. I was here, in Kona, about to conquer the most difficult race conceivable. The moment felt magic.

Then the cannon sounded and all hell broke loose. Arms and legs flew about as the water erupted into a boil. People have come away from the swim leg of a triathlon with broken noses. For that reason I pushed over toward the edge. Although my line resulted in a bit of a longer swim, moving outside of the scrum allowed me to stay clear of trouble. However, I was nearly undone by the initial flood of adrenaline that came over me. I knew I needed to pace myself, but I found I started out so fast that I was gasping for air by the time I reached the turnaround point. *This is ridiculous. Calm down!* I told myself. The little pep talk worked. I found a rhythm on the swim back in to shore. Small fish darted beneath me while little waves helped push me toward shore. I came out of the water in one hour, seven minutes. I looked up at my time and grinned. "We're looking good!" I said to Johnno and David as they carried me to my bike. I felt confident that I would have no trouble completing the course well under the cut-off times.

Then I discovered why the Hawaiian Ironman is like no other race in the world. The Hawaiian paradise became the closest thing to hell on earth one can experience without encountering a little horned man dressed in red carrying a pitchfork.

The bike leg takes place on the Queen Kaahumanu Highway, a hilly road that cuts through ancient lava fields. The black volcanic rock absorbs and intensifies the sun's heat. Since my handcycle seat sits down close to the pavement, the bike leg felt like riding 112 miles through an oven. The sun beat down from above, giving me a severe sunburn on my arms and the back of my neck. Normally a breeze would be a welcome relief, but not on the Queen K. The trade winds whip up the heat, making it even more intense. I'd been told to prepare for the heat, but I never anticipated the severity of the winds. Not long after I pedaled out onto the Queen K, the winds gusted up to sixty miles per hour right in my face. I had to use my lowest gear to make any progress, even when going downhill. Athletes flew past me, many of them shouting out, "Good job. Keep at it." I tried, but the wind and the heat coupled with the fatigue of using nothing but my arms took their toll.

After five hours I finally reached the turnaround at the halfway point. That's when I discovered another of Kona's secrets. The trade winds make a 180-degree switch in the early afternoon. I had counted on riding the tailwinds, but instead I faced the same sixty-mile-per-hour headwinds going back that I faced riding out. The locals said these were the worst winds in over ten years. I just happened to be lucky enough to have them hit the one year I planned on conquering the Ironman. My arms burned as I tried to keep the pedals circling round and round. More racers passed me. The confidence I felt when I got out of the water had long since blown away with the wind. I glanced over toward the ocean. The sun kept sinking lower and lower in the sky. I knew it would dip below the horizon at 5:30, which was also the cut-off time for the bike leg. Doubt washed over me.

By midafternoon my doubts grew. I became fairly certain that I could not finish the bike leg in the allotted time. Occasionally I caught sight of Johnno, David, and Don out on the course waving little Australian flags. At first, seeing them gave me a burst of energy, but by the end of the day not even Don's big grin could lift my spirits. I could barely force my arms to continue pushing the pedals. I was spent. I made up my mind that if I missed the cut-off time, I was done. My race was over.

By the time I reached the last hill about half a mile from the transition zone, I knew it was over. The sun had set and so had my dream of becoming the first wheelie to complete the Ironman. As I started up the last hill I spotted Johnno. He'd sprinted out across a golf course to meet me. At first he walked along beside me and didn't say a word as I strained to push myself up one more hill. Finally, he broke the silence. "Mate, you missed the cut-off time, and you've been disqualified. But they're going to let you go on and do the marathon. They want you to finish the race."

I did not say a word for a long time. I kept pushing on the pedals, slowly moving up the steep hill. I knew he thought he was bringing me a mixed bag of both good and bad news—the bad news being that I wouldn't officially finish, but the good news was I could torture my body with 26.2 miles in my racing chair after more than ten hours of abusing every muscle in my upper body. I looked at my legs and grew angry that they could not push me on a bike like every other athlete. But then I reminded myself that if my legs worked, I probably would not have been in Kona to begin with.

After what felt like an eternity of silence, Johnno spoke again. He knew what I was thinking. He could see I was feeling sorry for myself, which is never a good thing. "John, you've got to go on," he said. "Today is my son's birthday, but I came here to support you." He paused for a moment. "You've got to go on," he said again, not pleading but ordering. I looked up at Johnno. Even in the dying light I could see tears in his eyes. "You're going to have to give a bit more," he said.

"Okay," I replied. I could not do otherwise. If I stopped now, I wasn't giving up on myself but on Johnno and everyone else who made this day happen.

I pedaled into the transition zone where race president David Yates waited for me. "I'm sorry, John, but you're forty minutes late," he said. "We have to disqualify you. But we would like you to continue anyway to see whether this course can be completed by a wheelchair athlete."

"Okay. I'm going on," I said. I didn't want to continue. My arms screamed at me in pain. Rather than give in to them I let Johnno and David lift me from my handcycle onto my racing chair. For the first few moments I just sat there, exhausted. Finally I pushed myself onto the marathon course and out into the dark. Glow sticks hung from my chair while two motorcycle escorts lit my way.

My resolve to keep going took a blow when I hit the first hill. It felt like a sheer cliff face. I pushed down hard on the rims, trying to force my chair up the hill, but the front wheel popped up and nearly caused me to flip over backward. Now I was stuck. I could not move. If I couldn't move, I couldn't finish. David and Johnno walked alongside me. "I'm sorry, guys," I apologized, "but I just can't do it."

"What if you turned the chair around and backed up the hill?" David suggested. Honestly, my first inclination was to tell him to climb in the chair and try it himself. But I didn't. I pulled off my gloves so that I could grip the rims, turned the chair around, and slowly backed up the hill. When I reached the crest, I thought someone was playing a cruel joke on me. Another hill just as steep lay just ahead. I tried to gain as much momentum going down the first hill that I could, but it ran out halfway up the next. I stopped, defeated. Johnno and David caught up to me. "I'm not enjoying this anymore," I said. This was my way of saying I was done.

Johnno leaned over to me and said with a wry smile, "The pain won't last forever, but the memories will."

"Get that on film, brothers," I said to the film crew from NBC covering the event. "That was beautiful." I then spun my chair around and backed up the hill. From the moment Johnno spoke those words, I knew there was no way I could possibly quit.

I finished the race in fourteen hours, fifty-two minutes. How did I suddenly find the resolve to keep going when I already knew I could not possibly wheel another inch? Johnno put it like this as I neared the finish line: "You went from Struggle Street to going again because it wasn't the hill that was stopping you—it was your mind." He was right. Once I refused to stop myself, I found the strength to keep going. The payoff was worth the pain. A huge crowd greeted me at the finish. I did a wheelie as I crossed the line, then pulled out an Australian flag and waved it. Girls leaned over the crowd barriers and kissed me. Don slipped a lei around my neck, which had to suffice because I did not qualify for a finisher's medal. With that, my race was over. I had accomplished my goal. I was an Ironman.

Only I knew I wasn't.

I thought I never wanted to see Kona again. I never wanted to subject my body to that kind of pain again. But one year later I was back to finish what I had started. Unfortunately, I didn't. A flat tire on my handcycle caused me to miss the cutoff by fifteen minutes in 1996. I went ahead and did the marathon leg anyway, finishing the race in fourteen hours, thirty-nine minutes. The officials at the finish line slipped a finisher's medal around my neck. Grasping it, I thought to myself, *Mission accomplished. I am never coming back*. However, once we got back to the hotel Don looked at me and said, "You have to give that medal back."

"What are you talking about?" I argued. "I earned this."

"You didn't finish within the qualifying times for the bike cut-off. You won't be able to live with yourself if you keep it."

"You're touched in the head," I said.

By the next morning I knew Don was right. I went to the race director, Sharron Ackles, and handed her the medal. Tears flooded her eyes. "Oh, John," she said, "if anyone deserves this medal, it's you!"

"But I didn't earn it, Sharron," I replied. "When I earn it, believe me, I will never turn loose of it. But for now, you need to take this back."

Reluctantly, she did. However, the seed was planted. I knew it was not a question of if but when I would earn a finisher's medal outright.

One year later I returned to Kona. This time I came equipped with a new, lighter handcycle and it paid off. Nineteen ninety-seven was the first year that there was an official wheelchair category. Two other wheelies also qualified for Kona. Now I not only had to finish each leg in the allotted times, but I had to beat the other guys. My goal was not to be the second wheelchair athlete to finish the Hawaiian Ironman. I was determined to be the first.

Twelve hours, twenty-one minutes after the start cannon sounded, I crossed the finish line within the set qualifying times and finally earned my finisher's medal. The other two wheelies were far behind me. I'd accomplished a goal I'd set for myself three years earlier. That night I collapsed on the bed in the hotel room I shared with my brother Don. I lay there, reflecting on what had just happened. I was an Ironman. I had conquered the most difficult endurance race imaginable. It may have taken me three tries, but I never gave up and I never gave in. I now felt that I was the equal of any athlete in the world.

"Hey, Don," I called out in the dark.

"What, John?" Don said, tired and annoyed.

"What do you think about doing the English Channel next year?"

Don told me to do something that is anatomically impossible, but I knew he was in. I'd climbed one Everest. Now it was time to go conquer the next.

5

More than Able, Part 2

Looking back at Kona, I saw it as more than a goal accomplished. All the pieces of my life up to that point fit together perfectly to create that final result. As I wrote in the preface, I am convinced nothing happens by chance. When my legs did not respond in the months after my accident, I turned my attention to my upper body. Without realizing it at the time, my "wasted" efforts on legs that refused to respond were actually the perfect exercise routine to prepare me for triathlons. If I had not spent those two years building my upper body, I never would have qualified for Kona, much less become the first wheelie to complete it.

The right people have also come into my life at just the right times. When I lost my spot on the Penrith Panthers under-23 team, I was devastated. Going to the Warragamba Wombats felt like a huge step backward. But if I had not gone to Warragamba, I never would have met my teammate John Young. After my accident, no one came to the hospital more than Johnno, and after my release, he and I became the best of friends as well as workout partners. We pushed one another beyond what either of us could have done on our own. If not for Johnno, I might have sunk down into the depths of self-pity and never moved on and had the success I did.

A chance meeting at the pool in Penrith not long after the 1995 Hawaiian Ironman was another instance of the right person coming into my life at just the right time. At first, I did not recognize the man who came over and introduced himself to me. But he recognized me and wanted to meet me. "Hi, John; I'm Ian Byrne. I've read about your sporting achievements," he said. "I just wanted to compliment you on a job well done."

As soon as I heard his name, I knew I was the one who should be handing out compliments. Ian had been in all the papers, having just swum the English Channel at the age of forty-seven. "I'm honored to meet you," I said. "I read about your swimming the channel, and I have to say I am very impressed. Well done, mate."

"Thanks," Ian said. "But you know," he added, "if I can do it, then surely a fit, young, and motivated guy like you can too." I don't know what prompted Ian to throw down that challenge. I'm not even sure he was completely serious at the time. However he meant it, the seed was planted. *If I can do it, then surely a fit, young, and motivated guy like you can too.* The words turned over and over in my mind for a very long time. I knew Ian wasn't just handing out an empty compliment. He truly believed that if he could conquer the channel, then surely a man who had completed the Hawaiian Ironman could too. I was struck by the fact that Ian said this to me as though he didn't even notice my wheels. He spoke to me as one extreme athlete to another. *If I can do it, then surely a fit, young, and motivated guy like you can too.* Fit and motivated, not disabled. I liked Ian from the start.

Our conversation went on for a bit after that. I peppered him with questions about what the experience was like. He answered them all, which only made me more curious. By the time we parted I was hooked on the idea of swimming the channel.

After that "chance" meeting with Ian, I started doing a little research into the history of channel swims. On August 25, 1875, Captain Matthew Webb became the first man to successfully swim from England to France without the use of artificial aids. Afterward, he famously said, "Nothing great is easy." His words sounded like a personal challenge for me to come give it a try. I also learned that only about 10 percent of those who attempt the swim succeed. It's not that they all just run out of gas. Weather conditions can be treacherous, and they change quickly. Many endurance swimmers find themselves driven backward by the wind and waves. It is as though nature doesn't want to surrender the channel on those days. I also discovered that no wheelchair athlete had ever successfully made the swim. As if that were not enough motivation, I also learned one little fact that caused me to set my sites squarely on swimming the channel: no athlete of any kind had ever completed the Hawaiian Ironman *and* swum the English Channel. *That's it*, I told myself after I finally finished the Ironman in 1997. *I will be the first.*

People have asked what it is like to swim the English Channel. Anyone can re-create the conditions at home. Simply fill a very large washing machine with several bags of ice, add a little salt, top it off with water, then strap it to a roller coaster, and climb inside and flail around for thirteen hours or so. Make sure the washing machine is set to high.

You may think I am kidding, but if anything, a washing machine filled with ice water on a roller coaster undersells the experience. Nothing can fully prepare you for the conditions you will face when the channel decides to take you for a spin. Five hours into my first attempt to swim the twenty-one miles from Dover to Calais on August 17, 1998, the winds began to pick up to force 5 on the Beaufort Wind Scale, which relates not only to wind speeds but also to the size of the swells the wind produces. The higher the number, the stronger the wind, the bigger the waves, and the crazier someone has to be to swim in it. Force 5 is a wind between eighteen and twenty-four miles per hour and swells over six feet in height. Six hours into my swim, they hit force 6 directly in my face—that is, they kicked up to between twenty-four and thirty-one miles per hour, which whipped up nine- and ten-foot swells. Nine hours in, the wind hit force 7 (up to thirty-eight miles per hour), with gusts at force 8 (or around forty-five miles per hour), creating a swell nearly big enough to hide a house. Nothing I did in training prepared me for that. I don't think anything can.

As soon as I decided I would indeed attempt the channel, I sought out legendary Australian distance swimmer Des Renford. Des swam the channel so many times people started calling him the "Calais Commuter." Between 1970 and 1980, Des successfully crossed the channel nineteen times. On his first attempt, he tried a double crossing. He almost made it back to Dover when a wave threw him into the hull of his support vessel, dislocating his shoulder. Even then, Des kept on until his support team forced him to stop.

Des was not encouraging initially. "I'm not sure you know what you are getting yourself into," Des said to me when I told him my intentions. "The channel is unlike any other body of water in the world. One minute it can be as flat as a carpet, the next you're on top of twenty-foot waves."

Undeterred, I kept pressing him for more information about the swim. The worst news he shared was that the Channel Swimming Association (CSA), which sanctions all official attempts, does not allow wet suits. "Captain Webb didn't have a wet suit, and anyone who tries to replicate what the captain did can't wear one either," I was told. This presented a bit of a challenge. Because my legs do not work, they are little more than dead weight in the water. Left to themselves they will eventually pull me down. When the CSA consented to my request to swim the channel (by a 3–2 vote), they made one concession for my condition. They allowed me to strap a small flotation device between my legs to keep them upright.

Once I received permission to attempt a swim, I threw myself into training. Two more people came into my life at this very strategic time, people without whom the swim would not have been possible. The first was David Knight, who was then the managing director for Gatorade in Australia. David and I first met in 1996 at the Noosa Triathlon on the Queensland Sunshine Coast. Gatorade was one of the sponsors of the event, and David came to meet a number of leading triathletes over sponsorship dinners. The two of us hit it off from the start. However, we didn't see each other again until I happened upon him sitting on the steps of the Sydney Opera House with his wife and children, watching the start of a test race for the upcoming Sydney Olympics triathlon course. We started talking about the Noosa Triathlon. He told me I had inspired him to get in shape and do the 1997 event. "I'll do it with you, mate," I said. I kept my promise. The night after the 1997 race, David was riding a high from actually finishing. The two of us started talking about what we were going to do next. "I'm planning on swimming the English Channel," I announced to him. "And what are you going to do?"

David hesitated before finally blurting out, "I'm going to do the Hawaiian Ironman."

"I can help get you ready for it, if you like," I said.

He liked the idea. Then he said, "I want to help you with the channel swim. And I think I may be able to get Gatorade to sponsor you."

That was a godsend. Training for the channel became my full-time job. Over the course of eight months, I swam over 1,100 miles.

With Gatorade on board as a sponsor, I was free to throw myself fully into my training without worrying about how I might support myself. Gatorade was not the first or only company to step up for me. Through my brother Don's efforts, Nike sponsored me as an athlete. I don't know if I fully realized it at the time, but my boyhood dream of becoming a professional athlete had come true. When Nike learned of my channel attempt, they gave me a $20,000 grant to use for the charity of my choice. This seed led to probably the greatest accomplishment of my life, but more on that later.

David did more than bring Gatorade on board as a sponsor. The two of us became close friends. He even agreed to join me on my swim as one of my support swimmers. The CSA allows two support swimmers who can spend up to an hour at a time in the water swimming alongside those attempting the crossing. Support swimmers lift the swimmers' spirits and keep them going. They cannot, however, do anything to physically aid in the attempt. With David so fully invested in my endeavor, Gatorade upped their support as well. They funded a documentary of my channel swim. A camera crew came along on several of my training swims, then followed me to England for the actual crossing.

Thanks to Gatorade's sponsorship, I started a regimen of marathon swim training. I was fortunate to live a couple of miles from the Penrith Lakes complex. The man-made lakes formed a three-mile loop where I could swim as long as I needed to without stopping. I started in the summer months when the water was quite pleasant for a swim. Each day I did lap after lap, gradually increasing my time in the water to four hours, then well beyond. Spending so much time in the water is, to say the least, quite boring, especially alone. I was fortunate when another accomplished athlete and friend, Wally Brumniach, volunteered to swim with me. He worked for a life coach named Maurie Rayner. Wally is, I believe, the most positive-thinking, optimistic person I know. He didn't just keep me company. He helped shape my thinking as I tackled one of the greatest sporting challenges on the planet. I called the channel my next Everest, but in truth, four times as many people have climbed Everest as have swum the channel. Perhaps Everest climbers should call the mountain their English Channel.

Through the week I swam primarily at the Penrith Lakes. On weekends I headed off to the beach with David Knight. Susie Maroney, a professional marathon swimmer and the first Australian to complete a double crossing of the channel, even joined me for a couple of my training swims. Sydney boasts some of the most beautiful and famous beaches in the world. Bondi sits atop that list. While most tourists and locals go there for a little dip or some surfing, I went out beyond the normal swimming area. Bondi is a bit of a bay with two points sticking out on either end. The bay is just under a mile wide between the two points. I swam lap after lap between those two points. David Knight or one of my other friends often joined me. In the summer months, the sea and the sun felt wonderful. But as winter set in and the water temperature dropped, the experience was not quite as pleasant. Yet swimming in cold water was exactly what I needed to do to acclimate myself to the conditions I would face in the channel. Even in the middle of summer, the water temperature between England and France never reaches sixty degrees. During one of my training swims at the Penrith Lakes, the water had dipped down to forty-eight. The channel felt absolutely balmy in comparison. The extra fifty pounds of fat I packed on in the months before I left for England helped protect me from the cold as well.

When I first looked out upon the English Channel from Dover, I felt very, very small and ill prepared. Off in the distance I could just make out a landmass I knew was France. The twenty-one miles between it and me never looked longer. I took a deep breath. If only I could be so lucky as to make it across by only swimming twenty-one miles. Because of the swift ocean currents flowing from north to south, most attempts cover nearly double that amount. At least I would not make the journey alone. My brother Don flew over with his two children. My sister Marion came over along with David Knight; Wally Brumniach and his wife; my swim coach, David Harvey; George Lawlor from Nike; photographers; and the documentary video crew. Perhaps the most important person on my team was a man I met in Dover. Reg Brickell was the captain of the *Viking Princess*, the fishing boat that would serve as my support vehicle. Channel swimmers don't just dive in the water and have a go at it. A support vessel, usually a fishing boat, guides the swimmer along, keeping us on course and informing of changing conditions.

After two weeks in England waiting for word of when I would get my chance, we were told on August 15 that my turn would come in two days. Because the boat was small, most of my crew had to stay behind in Dover. David Knight, David Harvey, Wally, George Lawlor, and I got into the *Viking Princess* for the short ride up the coast to the official starting point. David Knight and Wally came as my support swimmers. David Harvey covered me with wool fat, the only provision against the cold water (besides the extra pounds I packed on). Under CSA rules I could not be carried out into the sea. Instead, I made my way up to the high-water mark on the beach, turned around, and did a long bum shuffle (sitting on the sand, supported by my arms, I'd shuffle—arms, bum, arms, bum) across pebbles and rocks into the water. Even though I had trained in cold water back home, the fifty-nine-degree waters of the North Atlantic jolted my system, kicking my adrenaline into high gear.

I thought I had learned how little of life we truly control after my accident on the M4. The channel retaught me this lesson with a vengeance. Through the first several hours of my swim, conditions were okay. The seas had a bit of chop to them, but not enough to keep me from my goal. But then the winds began to pick up. And pick up. And pick up some more. At the six-hour mark the gusting winds hit thirty-five miles per hour. Ten-foot swells tossed me about. They even threatened the helicopter carrying the documentary camera crew as it dipped low for footage of my swim. Reg tried to protect me by angling his ship to absorb the brunt of the waves before they crashed into me. On board the *Viking Princess* seasickness reigned. Reg told David Harvey, "I think he should pack it in."

David Knight conveyed the word to me. After swimming 1,100 training miles and devoting eight months of my life to this attempt, I wasn't about to stop because of a little chop. "I've come this far; I don't want to give up now," I said. I did not realize that the wind was blowing me back toward England faster than I could push myself toward France. Undeterred, I pressed on, but the waves were relentless. Swells picked me up then dumped me back down under the water. I came up, disoriented. After dog-paddling for a moment to get my bearings, I took off swimming again only to repeat this game over and over for the next three hours.

Nine hours into my swim Reg came over to the railing and delivered the bad news. "Johnny, you've been going backwards for the past couple of hours. It's over. It's not you. It's the conditions. No one is going to get across today."

I nodded my assent. I had no choice. No matter how determined I might have been, no matter how hard I tried, the channel was not going to be beaten on this day. My guys lifted me up into the boat for a very cold, quiet, bumpy ride back to England.

After I failed to make it across the channel, all of my support team, with the exception of David Harvey, my coach, went back to their lives. The camera crew went home to Australia, while Don flew home to Canada and David Knight went away for a vacation with his family. David Harvey and I stayed behind in England hoping for another chance. I could not give up this easily.

Two weeks later my second chance arrived. Reg called, telling me I could give it a go on August 30. "Meet me on the dock at four a.m. We're going to get an earlier start this time," he said.

The sea cooperated on my second attempt. However, the real problem I ran into involved my support team's schedules. Don dropped everything and came over in time to catch a place on the *Viking Princess*, as did the documentary film crew. Wally returned as one of my support swimmers, but David Knight was on a skiing holiday on the other side of the world with his family. I called to let him know about my second attempt, full well knowing he would have to miss it. "What are you talking about?" David said. "I'm on my way."

David was not there when I did the bum shuffle down the sand and pebbles into the channel for my second attempt. I started an hour earlier to give myself extra time in case of any weather surprises. I also had a faster start. On my first attempt some of the wool fat smeared across my goggles. I wasted a lot of time trying to clean them in the water before giving up and getting a second pair. On my second attempt I didn't have any such delay. I also took fewer food breaks. The first time across I took liquid food and Gatorade every twenty minutes or so. If that seems a bit excessive, you've never tried swimming across twenty-one miles of open ocean. You burn a lot of calories even in calm seas. For my second attempt we cut the breaks down to once an hour. Once I was far enough along that it appeared I would make it, we increased the frequency just a bit.

While I swam through the ink-black water in the early morning dark of Dover, David Knight was running between planes, hurrying to England. He called me from Bangkok before my swim. "I'm changing planes, but I will be there. I'll hire a helicopter at Heathrow and have them drop me in the channel next to you if I need to," he said. Both of us knew that couldn't happen, but David's determination to be with me on this swim was as great, if not greater, than my determination to conquer the channel.

He did not hire a helicopter when he reached England. Instead, he rushed up and down the docks at Dover, looking for a fishing boat willing to take him out to find me. Keep in mind, the channel may look small on a map, but it is a big body of water. Trying to find a little fishing trawler like the *Viking Princess* puttering alongside a single man in the water is next to impossible. No one would take David until he finally found one boat with an equally reluctant crew. "I've got a mate and he's in a wheelchair and he's swimming the channel and I have to find him!" They looked at him like he'd lost his mind. However, their mood changed when he pulled several hundred pounds out of his wallet. "You can buy a lot of fish with this," he pleaded. The crew agreed. David had his boat.

I knew none of this as I splashed about in the cold waters of the English Channel. David Harvey and Wally shouted encouragement to me. "You're making good time. Keep at it." Time, however, was not on my side. Nor is it ever on the side of a channel swimmer. If I was to make it to France, I had to make it across the current before it shifted in the late afternoon and swept me back toward England. David Harvey and Wally alternated swimming alongside me, an hour at a time. I was feeling the ocean, feeling the pain of a shoulder I had partially separated in the 1995 Ironman that had never fully healed, feeling just a bit out of gas, when for some reason I looked up at the *Viking Princess* for one of the first times that day. "Hello, mate," David Knight said, looking down at me, a huge grin on his face.

I've got the best friends in the world, I thought to myself. I put my head down in the water and started swimming again. My shoulder no longer ached. My arms felt lighter. There was no way I would fail on this day.

Twelve hours and fifty-five minutes after my bum shuffle down into the water, I did another bum shuffle up the beach in France. With the current washing me down the channel as I swam, I had covered over thirty miles in the water, not including the miles I swam on my first attempt two weeks earlier. Even after thirty miles, I had covered several more yards before my swim that could be counted as official. According to the rules, I was not completely across the channel until I completely cleared the water line. I scooted along on my bum, my friends standing to the side, cheering and clapping for me. I'd been told to make sure I pick up a souvenir of my journey, so I reached down and picked up a rock from the French shore and stuffed it into my Speedo. A little farther up the shore I found another and saved it as well. Closer to the water line I found another that looked appealing, so I shoved it down my Speedo with the other two. When I finally reached dry land, I fell back on my back.

Once I had made it above the water line, the film crew came over. "How do you feel?"

"Sometimes you win and sometimes you lose," I said, "but I hope today I've won for all the boys and girls around the world in wheelchairs. If they need someone to look up to, hopefully they've got someone to look up to now." I said this because I had a lot of time to think out in the water and I had figured out where I needed to invest the $20,000 Nike gave me. A few months after I returned to Australia I started the John Maclean Foundation through the New South Wales Wheelchair Sports Association. At the time, I wanted the association to identify one boy or girl who was having trouble pursuing their sport because they couldn't afford the specialized equipment they needed. Then, at an annual banquet, I would present them with a check. It was very low-key and low-maintenance. At the time, that seemed to be enough.

6

Some Dreams Don't Need to Come True

Two years and one month after triumphantly bum-shuffling up the beach in Wissant, France, I found myself lying on the ground in front of 115,000 people, my racing chair on top of me. One wheel spun round and round in front of my face as if the race could still be won. A collective gasp had gone up when my chair flew over onto one side, spilling me out onto the track of Sydney's Olympic stadium. The sound was quite a contrast from the deafening roar that had greeted me when I was introduced prior to the race. While few in attendance knew who I was, I represented Australia, and that was enough to make the home crowd go nuts. Now they stared at me in shocked silence while the other seven competitors charged toward the finish. Even the man with whom I had collided kept going without going down.

I wanted help to get my chair upright and finish the race, but the Olympic officials wouldn't hear of it. "We need to get you off the track," one said as he came over to me. I was partially on the track and partially on the infield just up from the javelin competition. I guess the Olympic officials didn't want to add insult to injury by taking the chance of an errant throw impaling me.

Not that I would have minded having a javelin rain down and put me out of my misery. This was, to put it mildly, one of the most humiliating moments of my life. My mind simply could not process what had just happened. Unlike my first failed attempt to cross the channel, I could not wait two weeks for a second chance to get it right. This race was my one shot in the Olympics. This 1,500-meter wheelchair race was a demonstration sport for only the second time in the history of the games. When other Olympians fail, they can at least console themselves knowing they might get another shot four years later. I didn't have that luxury. Yes, I had qualified for the Paralympics, which were to be held in the same stadium a couple of weeks later, but that was not the same. I was one of only sixteen wheelchair Olympians in these games, and I would have the distinction of being the only one with the letters DNF (did not finish) permanently inscribed next to my name. To make matters worse, the two athletes who trailed me at the time of my crash on the last lap went on to finish first and second.

As I lay on the track, a strong sense of déjà vu came over me. I couldn't help but think that I was meant to crash and spoil my Olympic dreams, as if lying on the track in disgrace was my destiny. A slight unbelieving smile came over my face. *Wow, this is really happening,* I thought to myself.

Race officials helped me up and ushered me off the track. A reporter came rushing over, microphone in hand. "How are you feeling, John, after the crash?"

I didn't feel like being honest. I did not want to blurt out all my frustration in front of an audience of hundreds of millions around the world. So I fell back on a few well-worn clichés used by failing athletes throughout time. I imagine that the first guy to trip and fall in the original Olympics in ancient Greece probably said about the same thing when asked how he felt. "It's not the result I was looking for, but these things are part of the sport," I said. Then I added, "Now I'm just looking forward to the Paralympic Games and doing the best I can."

The sour taste of failure had not faded when the Paralympics rolled around. I had qualified in the 1,500 meters; 5,000 meters; 10,000 meters; the marathon; and the 4 x 400 relay, all of which would be run in the span of just a few days. Between heats, semifinals, and finals, I raced at least once a day, every day. A couple of days in I knew I was in serious trouble. Not only did I not feel like getting back out on the track after my embarrassment in the Olympic race, but racing so often in the Paralympics meant I was already exhausted before the starter's pistol even fired. My inexperience as a wheelchair racer was showing. Looking back, I should have focused on one or two events, but I thought qualifying for so many guaranteed my spot on the team and gave me that many more chances to medal. The closest I came to the podium was a tenth-place finish in the marathon. The low point of the Paralympic Games came in the 5,000-meter semifinals where I not only crashed again, but the judges reviewed the tape and disqualified me. DNF next to my name was bad enough. DQ was the ultimate humiliation.

That I had even qualified for the Olympic and Paralympic teams should have been accomplishment enough. Most athletes not only focus on one or two specific events in their sport and work to be the best in those, but they normally pick a single sport to which they devote all their time and energy. Not me. To me, sports are a bit like walking up to an ice cream stand. No one wants to go to a place that serves only vanilla. Even thirty-one flavors is a little tame for my taste. While I certainly have my favorite—rum raisin, of course—I cannot imagine a world where it's all rum raisin all the time. Nor could I ever see confining myself to one sport.

I'm always drawn to whatever door may open, and once I walk through I push myself to see how far I can go.

The dream of finding a way to compete in the Sydney Games came to me as soon as I heard that the Olympic and Paralympic Games would be held right in my backyard. And I do mean right in my backyard. I watched the Olympic stadium go up as I traveled up and down the M4 between my Penrith home and Sydney. As I mentioned earlier, the rowing center was even closer, perhaps a mile from my front door. I trained there for the channel swim while they constructed the grandstands at the finish line. These were to be the first games held in Australia since the Melbourne Games of 1956, and the entire country was quite excited by it all, especially the area in and around Sydney. I, too, found myself caught up in the excitement. However, unlike most of my compatriots, I didn't just want to go watch the games. I wanted to be a part of them.

I first toyed with the idea of qualifying for the Paralympics in 1995 when I took up the sport of wheelchair basketball. I was chosen for the train-on squad for the 1996 Atlanta Games, but I gave up the sport when I realized I had unfinished Ironman business in Kona to which I needed to attend. The idea of representing Australia in the Paralympics never really went away, nor did the desire for a gold medal. I won my first gold at the age of twelve in the 1,500-meter racewalking national championships. All the accolades lit a fire inside of me, one that only grew as I did. The thought of going for the gold again on a much bigger stage very much appealed to me.

Unfortunately, Paralympians have far fewer sports from which to choose than do prospective Olympians. The triathlon, which is an Olympic event but not yet Paralympic, would have been my obvious choice if it were available. However, since it was not, wheelchair racing seemed the logical move. I had spent a lot of time in my wheelchair competing in triathlons around the world, and I thought I could adapt to focusing on only the one discipline pretty quickly. I met a coach named Jenni Banks who agreed to train me. "You face an uphill battle," she warned. "The approach and strategy is completely different from what you are used to. Most of the people against which you will compete have been at this a long time. I'm not sure you can get up to speed with them in such a short time."

"I think I'm up to the challenge," I replied. I didn't mean it in a boastful way. I simply knew myself and what I had done in the past. I'd never tried a swim longer than the 2.4-mile Ironman swim before setting my sights on the English Channel. Eight months later I swam over thirty miles of open ocean. I was still riding the high of making it to France. I figured if I could turn myself into a long-distance swimmer, I could build on the skills I'd honed in triathlons and learn to compete in wheelchair racing.

Jenni was less confident than I was. "The Oz Day 10K is in a couple of weeks at the Rocks.* If you can do that in under twenty-seven minutes, give me a call."

The Oz Day was not just any 10K. Every year it helped mark the Australia Day celebration. Elite wheelchair racers came from all over the world to compete in it. Kicking off my racing career against such a field was going to be a real baptism by fire. I had hoped to compete in the race as just another wheelie without drawing attention to myself, but the sporting profile I had developed after the Hawaiian Ironman and the channel swim caught the

---

* The Rocks, the site of the first English settlement in Australia, is a popular tourist area near the base of the Sydney Harbour Bridge and a short walk from the opera house.

attention of the press and reporters were keen to talk to me. You must keep in mind that we Aussies are very much into sports, and not just our team sports. With a population of just under 24 million, when one of us does something remarkable on the world stage, the entire country takes notice. So when word got out that John Maclean, the first paraplegic to conquer the Hawaiian Ironman and swim the English Channel, had taken up wheelchair racing, it was a somewhat newsworthy event.

I didn't care about generating publicity one way or another. All the publicity in the world wouldn't help me finish the Oz 10K in under twenty-seven minutes, and that's what I had to do if I had any shot at all of qualifying for Sydney the next year. On the day of the race, I poured everything I had into those ten kilometers and finished with a time just a tick under twenty-six minutes. Overall, I finished tenth out of a field of fifty. I thought that wasn't too bad for a first effort. However, my race drew even more attention than I anticipated, all because of something that happened at the finish. Coming down the homestretch, I was so intent on holding off a Canadian competitor rushing up beside me that I did not notice the rapidly approaching finish line. I lowered my head, putting all my strength into every push down on the wheels. As I flew across the finish line, I looked up just in time to see the barrier just beyond the line. My chair crashed into it at full speed, crushing the front forks and snapping off the front wheel. I, however, was completely unharmed. I never imagined my first race might be an omen of what was to come.

Over the next eighteen months I trained for the games full-time. I traveled all over the world trying to establish qualifying times in as many events as I could. My entry into the sport and the interest surrounding me did not endear me to others in the wheelchair racing community. Most of these guys had devoted their sporting lives to this sport. Many viewed me as an interloper. I was taken aback by some of the criticism I received, as well as the cold shoulders from some. In triathlons, the camaraderie between athletes feels like family, win or lose. That wasn't the case in the world of wheelchair racing. Nevertheless, many of the top racers became my good friends. I trained together with a few and sought advice from those with much more experience than me. The work paid off. By the end of April 2000, I had qualifying times in the 1,500 meters; 5,000 meters; 10,000 meters; marathon; and 4 x 400 meter relay.

That's when I received a phone call from Chris Nunn, the coach of the Australian athletics team, telling me about the 1,500-meter Olympic demonstration event. "Are you interested?" he asked.

"Are you kidding?" I said. "Of course I am!"

"I have to choose one athlete to represent Australia. It's between you, Paul Nunnari, and Kurt Fearnley."

Paul, a young wheelchair racer at the time, and I trained together and had formed a close friendship. I knew Kurt to be an up-and-comer in the world of wheelchair racing. (He later went on to win the Paralympic gold in 2004 and 2008.) "Whatever method you choose to select the spot I'm sure will be fair," I told Chris. I felt honored to even be in the conversation after such a short time in the sport.

A few months later it was announced that the meet in Delémont, Switzerland, was chosen as the qualification race for the Olympic 1,500. There were four heats and two semifinals. The top three semifinalists from each race along with the next two fastest times would go on to compete against one another in Sydney. Paul, Kurt, and I all took part. I didn't want to take a chance of having to sweat out whether or not I was one of the next two fastest. I had to finish in the top three to punch my ticket to Sydney. Kurt and I both made it out of our heats into the semis, but Paul did not. Racing is like that. Some days are just not your day.

Fortunately, this was my day. In my semifinal race I broke out to an early lead. I knew I didn't have the kick most of the others had. Getting out front and staying there was my only chance to finish in the top three. I led after the first lap. And the second. And the third. I held on to the lead through the halfway point of the last lap. My head down, pushing hard, someone flew around me. Twenty meters later, my head still down, pushing with all I had left, another chair flew past. I rounded the last turn, one hundred meters to go, still holding on to third place. I heard breathing behind me. I pushed that much harder. Out of the corner of my eye I saw the chair pull up nearly even as the finish line closed in on us. I gave my wheels one final push as I crossed the line. I looked around at the officials, but no signal came as to whom had taken third. Five minutes passed before the judges came down and rendered the official results. I had placed third by a whopping one–one hundredth of a second. I was going to Sydney.

After qualifying for the games, I kept training. However, I did not want to miss out on the national celebration of the games. My Olympic party started when I carried the Olympic torch through Penrith as part of the torch relay leading up to the games. I have to tell you, the elation of that moment felt like a victory lap before the races had even been run. Then I did television commercials for Nike and General Motors in Australia, both of which sponsored me at the time. The games themselves opened with the giant party that was the opening ceremonies. I was just happy to be a part of it all. Having qualified for the Olympics by the narrowest of margins, just being there felt like my gold medal.

Then came my race.

And the crash.

That split-second disaster came to define both my Olympic and Paralympic experience. Prior to the crash I was John Maclean, the first wheelie to complete the Hawaiian Ironman, the first to swim the English Channel, one of the top eight wheelchair racers in the world. Afterward, as I made my way through the Olympic Village, I saw people point and stare. I was simply that guy who crashed.

I did not handle this failure well, because it felt so much more final than my previous failures. I didn't meet all the cut-off times in my first two Hawaiian Ironman races, but still I finished, which was a victory in itself. My first channel crossing ended with me being hoisted up into my support ship, exhausted. But *I* had not failed. The weather won that day. No one could make it across in those conditions. I knew I would get another chance. Perhaps I could have adopted the same mindset this time and spent the next four years working toward the 2004 games in Athens. Somehow that never really entered my mind.

There was more at play than simply failing to medal in my first Paralympic Games. After the truck hit me on the M4, I used sports to regain my sense of self-worth. I threw myself into training and competing and pushing the limits of what a wheelchair athlete could do, all in an attempt to forever banish that image I caught of myself in the mirror not long after my accident. I loved the notoriety and the adulation sports provided. More than that, my accomplishments were, in my mind, my response to anyone who dared call me "disabled." I was more than able, and I planned to keep on proving it to anyone who doubted me.

Having so much of my self-worth tied up in my athletic achievements set me up for an inevitable fall. I didn't realize it until I found myself lying on the track in Sydney. In the weeks that followed I fell into a deep depression. David Knight tried to cheer me up. He reminded me of all I had accomplished just making it to Sydney. Perhaps, I thought, that was the problem. I should have been more focused on the gold, not satisfied in making the team. Such thoughts only made me kick myself even more for my failures. My friend's encouragement only made me that much more depressed.

I went back home to Penrith after the games and tried to hide from the world. I soon found that the world was not the problem. I was. I became very introspective. Not long after my release from the hospital in 1988 I married, but regrettably the marriage did not last. Many relationships followed, as I searched for my place in the world. Sitting alone in my house in Penrith, feeling the weight of my Olympic embarrassment, I also felt the weight of failed relationships. Additionally, I reflected on losing my mother. Even though I have only the vaguest of memories of her, I longed to be able to talk with her now to try to understand this emotional roller coaster.

With each passing day I sank deeper and deeper into this morass of introspection, regret, and despair. I knew something needed to change. I turned to my friend Wally Brumniach. He always told me what he thought, even if I didn't like what I needed to hear. "Mate, I'm in a bad place and I need someone to talk to," I said to him. Wally put me in contact with his friend Maurie Rayner. "Moses" was a life coach who ran a center in Victoria that focused on helping people confront their fears. He was also dying of bone cancer.

When I first walked in Maurie's front door, he greeted me by saying, "I'm dying and incapable of bullshit, so let's get on with it." I liked his directness. We sat down together in his office and over the next hour or so I told him my entire story. I talked about my early years in foster care and my mother's illness and suicide, my growing-up years in a working-class town, and my dreams of becoming an athlete someday. I took him through the entire story of my accident and my time in the hospital, as well as everything that followed—my failed marriage, the triathlons, the channel, and of course, the crash in front of 115,000 people in the Sydney Olympics. Maurie sat back and listened thoughtfully, never interrupting. He let me go on and on until I had nothing left to say.

Once I finally stopped talking, Maurie leaned forward, looked me squarely in the eyes, and said, "The best thing that ever happened to you was getting hit by that truck." I could not believe my ears. Had he been listening to what I said? "And the next best thing that ever happened to you was crashing at the Olympics. Maybe that will make you realize that life doesn't revolve around John Maclean."

I guess I should have become angry, but I did not. Deep down I knew Maurie was right. He now had my undivided attention. "Your feverish goal setting and the way you run from one challenge to the next have hindered your development as a person," he continued. "The answers you are looking for aren't going to be found in Hawaii or the English Channel or in the Olympic stadium. You're going to have to find them inside yourself."

Over the course of our weekend together, Maurie helped me look at my life from a completely different perspective. He opened my eyes to see my father's struggles in the aftermath of losing my mother. I came away with a new appreciation of both my father and my stepmother, whom he married when I was quite young. "If not for your accident, you might never have stopped and had to reflect on all of this," he told me. "All people are born with pure love in their hearts, John. But as we go through life, we start collecting 'yuck bits,' those unpleasant experiences, and we file them away in our heads. As we get older, those little 'yuck bits' add up, and it's my job to help you dissolve them."

I came away from my time with Maurie with a clearer mind about where I needed to go next. Maurie had asked me what I most wanted out of life. "A loving relationship," I told him. He also asked me how I wanted to be remembered. To my surprise, I suddenly realized the answer had nothing to do with sports or athletic accomplishments. More than anything, I wanted to make a contribution, to make a difference in the lives of others. I wanted people, especially kids, to understand that they could still achieve their dreams regardless of the cards life dealt them.

Over the next several months I reflected more and more on these two realizations. I came to understand that to accomplish either, I had to stop living my life for John Maclean and start living it for others. But after spending so much of my time and energy focused solely upon myself and my accomplishments, I wasn't sure where to start. Whatever it might be, I knew I was going to pour my whole self into it just as surely as I had given my all to Kona, the channel, and wheelchair racing. My father used to tell me, "John, it doesn't matter if you win or lose, just as long as you give it one hundred percent." I lived by that motto; however, I had always given my 100 percent to myself and my goals. Now it was time to think bigger.

7

Amanda

It wasn't love at first sight when I met Amanda, for either of us. She says when we first met, I wheeled into the room so disheveled that I looked like I needed someone to mother me. My shirt and pants badly needed to be ironed, and my curly, blond hair appeared to have a mind of its own. Given the circumstances, I probably should have done more to make a good first impression. Perhaps I should have come in a suit and tie, but at the time I didn't think that way. I was who I was, wrinkled clothes and all. And that's why I was there, to show who I really was. Amanda was the sales and marketing director of Murdoch Books in Sydney (a privately owned independent publisher), and I was there to pitch her, along with the company CEO and the publishing director, on the idea of publishing my autobiography. I'd started doing some speaking, and people kept asking if I had a book that told my story. When I told them I did not, they always replied, "You should. This would make a great book!" After hearing the same thing over and over again, I thought perhaps I should look into what it takes to get a book published. That's what took me to Murdoch Books that day. I wasn't looking for love—only a book deal.

The book deal came. I did not see Amanda again for nearly a

year, not until the book actually came out. Given her position with the company, Amanda rarely, if ever, personally handled the publicity of a single title. However, the publicist assigned to arrange my speaking engagements and book signings was out on maternity leave. Amanda volunteered to cover for her. She didn't do it because she was interested in me. She really just wanted the book to do well.

From the start the two of us worked well together. Neither of us harbored any romantic desires toward the other. The two of us were close in age, which automatically meant she wasn't the kind of woman I normally dated. She also wasn't all caught up in who I was and what I had done, which was a change from many of the women with whom I had become involved. That's not to say Amanda didn't appreciate my accomplishments. Obviously she did, or she never would have signed off on my book. But she wasn't in awe of me as a professional athlete, which was actually a breath of fresh air. I discovered pretty quickly that I could just be myself around her. I did not have to be John Maclean, the first wheelchair athlete to do whatever. I could just be me. She got me.

And I got her. She had a strength and confidence about her that I deeply respected. I'd never met a woman so comfortable in her own skin. The more we got to know each other, the more impressed I was by all she'd accomplished in her life. I think that is why our friendship worked so well. We both respected each other, and at the same time, we could be completely ourselves without trying to impress the other.

Once the book came out, Amanda and I saw quite a lot of each other. I found her very easy to talk to and I enjoyed her company. In fact, there were times when I had to go to an event or dinner that had nothing to do with the book, and I asked her to come along. She did the same with me. Neither of us thought of these as dates. That wasn't the kind of relationship we had at the time. We were building a friendship, one I felt quite lucky to have found. I don't know how my girlfriends at the time felt about her. To be honest, I never really gave it a lot of thought. I saw no reason for my romantic interests to feel threatened by my friendship with a smart, attractive, accomplished, independent woman. But then again, I am a guy with a less-than-stellar relationship track record. Understanding women has never been my strong suit. I even discussed my current relationships with Amanda to seek her advice. Like I said, I am not an expert on women.

Amanda and I kept in regular contact with each other for two and a half years. I cannot say constant contact, because both of us were quite busy in our careers. I took Maurie's advice to heart and expanded my athletic focus beyond myself. In 2002, prior to even thinking about writing a book, I handcycled from Brisbane to Melbourne, a distance of over 2,000 kilometers, or nearly 1,250 miles, to raise money and awareness for my foundation. Thanks to Maurie, I badly wanted to give back, and the John Maclean Foundation provided me with the perfect platform to do just that. My K4K ride, as we called it—that is, Kilometres for Kids—raised over $400,000. Like Maurie instructed me, this wasn't about John Maclean. Nor did the ride have anything to do with conquering any athletic challenge or winning any medals. Instead, the entire event was designed to open people's eyes to the needs of children confined to wheelchairs and to give people a way to do something to help.

The K4K ride corresponded with my expansion of the scope of my charity. When I first started the foundation, we provided grants to buy equipment for children in wheelchairs who wanted to pursue sports. With the K4K ride, the foundation opened the grants to any children in wheelchairs and their families, not just for sport equipment but for any of the multitude of expenses these families face when a child is confined to a chair. Every family with a child in a wheelchair for whatever reason faces financial challenges most people never consider. From the chairs themselves to vehicle conversions and home modifications, life for a family of a child with special needs is very, very expensive. Conditions like spinal muscular atrophy and accidents that rob children of the use of their legs strike without regard to a family's economic status. We give grants for chairs, both manual and powered, as well as grants toward modified vehicles and home modifications. At the time of this writing we have raised and distributed nearly four million dollars in Australia.

After training for the K4K ride for nearly a year, I kept on with handcycling in hopes of qualifying for the 2004 Athens Paralympic Games. I won the Australian national championship three years in a row, but that wasn't enough for me to make the national team. The selection committee went with athletes who had been at the sport much longer than I had. For me, trying to make the team was less about handcycling and more about seeing how far I could go if I really pushed myself. When I was selected to represent Australia in the 2004 games, my handcycling career came to an end. I also returned to the English Channel as David Knight's support swimmer in 2004. A year later David Wells and I completed the Molokai Challenge, a two-person open-ocean kayak event in Hawaii. Along the way I also competed in more Ironmans (although not Kona), and I went back to Hawaii to compete at the Ultraman World Championships, which is the equivalent of three Ironmans in three days. In between, I was inducted into the Hawaiian Ironman Hall of Fame, the first non-American so honored.

Amanda was also very busy in her work. Sometimes when I called her, she would be in London or New York or Frankfurt.

Even when she was back in Australia, it was hard for us to reconnect. She was very good at her job; a lot of her time was spoken for as a result. When we could not meet face-to-face, we kept in contact through calls and text messages. I did not realize it at the time, but my feelings for her had begun to grow beyond friendship. However, I was very hesitant to act, because I didn't want to do anything to jeopardize our friendship. Suffice it to say that I had been far less successful in my relationships than I had in sports. I could not bear the thought of losing Amanda's friendship if a romance did not work out.

Yet, the more time I spent with her, the more I realized we connected in a way I had never really connected with any other woman. My friends saw this before I did. One evening when Amanda and I were at a blues club, my close friend Hans leaned over to me and whispered, "Don't let this one get away." I wasn't quite sure what to do with Hans's advice. Romantically speaking, I didn't "have" her to let her get away. I just smiled at Hans and replied, "Duly noted."

My getting to know Amanda came at a time in my life where I was at a bit of a loss as to where I needed to concentrate my attention as an athlete. Now forty, I knew I had passed the age where my football career would have come to an end if the truck had never entered my life on the M4 in 1988. I started speaking more, something with which I was growing increasingly comfortable. I had always shared some of my story. Immediately after my accident Dr. John Yeo got me a job speaking for Spine-Safe, an in-school education program for kids that focused on safety and spinal injuries. I left Spine-Safe when my training for the Ironman consumed all my time. Through the years I spoke here and there. My presentations were a lot like my appearance at Murdoch Books: I wasn't exactly the most polished speaker on the podium. But the more I did it, the more I developed my own style that worked for me. The audiences seemed to enjoy it.

By the start of 2007 I began making plans to transition more into speaking as a way of making a living. Everything changed when Gary Foley, one of the wheelchair coaches I met in the lead-up to the Sydney Games, called me out of the blue. "Have you heard of a sport called adaptive rowing?" he asked.

"No," I replied.

"It is a new sport that has been included in the Paralympic program for the first time in Beijing next year."

"Okay."

"Do you want to give it a try?" Gary asked.

"Sure," I said without knowing any details. I'd seen rowers training on and off for years at the Sydney International Regatta Centre at Penrith Lakes. I had no idea exactly what adaptive rowing might involve, but if Gary thought I could do it, that was good enough for me.

"I hoped you would. The sport consists of two-person mixed teams, a man and a woman. The races are basically like what you've witnessed there in Penrith; however, the equipment is adapted to the user—in your case, trunk and arms," Gary explained.

"Okay. So what do I need to do?" I asked.

"There's a coach named Pedro Albisser at the regatta center that I want you to meet. He will take it from there."

I thanked Gary for thinking of me. The next day I drove ten minutes from my house to the lakes and introduced myself to Pedro. He was expecting me. "Where do I start?" I asked.

"I'll put you on a rowing machine and see if you can produce a result that shows you have some potential," Pedro replied. "Then we will go from there."

He strapped me onto the ergo machine and told me I needed

to clock a time of less than four minutes, twenty seconds for one kilometer to be considered for the training program. Even though this was my first time trying the sport, I came in at four minutes, ten seconds. Game on. Afterward there was only one question in my mind: "What do I need to do to win a gold medal?" For me, nothing else mattered. I knew what it took to compete in sports at an elite level. If I took this challenge, I faced at least eighteen months of intense training to which everything else in my life had to take a backseat. I'd competed in the games before. I had both Olympic and Paralympic experience. I'd been there, done that. If I went there again, it wasn't to experience the joy of wheeling into the opening ceremonies with the rest of the Australian team. From the start it was gold medal or bust.

"The first step is the state championships next weekend," Pedro explained. "You will compete in a single scull or boat. If you qualify, the nationals follow in six weeks. If you win your category there, and if there is a girl who wins hers and her times are good enough, you will go to the selection regatta and compete together. And if your times together are good enough, you will go on to the World Rowing Championships in Munich later this year, representing Australia. Then, if you make the finals, you will qualify the boat for Beijing. Any questions?"

"Let's get started," I said.

A week later I went to the state championships. I basically knew nothing about the sport in terms of techniques and strategy. The only thing really driving me was a burning desire to win a gold medal in Beijing. Pedro taught me as much as he could in a week, but there was only so much he could do. In spite of my inexperience, I finished second in the state championships, which was good enough to qualify for nationals. Six weeks later I won my event at nationals.

At the national tournament I met a young rower named Kathryn Ross, who was to become my partner in my quest for gold. Two people could not be more different than Kathryn and I, from our taste in music to the television shows we watch to the way we were brought up. However, once we were in the boat, Kathryn had what I call the giddyap factor. All her life she had been the girl in school who was always picked last for sporting teams, but she refused to let that hold her back. When the going gets tough, she gives it all she's got. Together with Pedro as our coach, I felt we had a gold-medal team.

After nationals, Kathryn stayed with me in Penrith for ten days to train together at the regatta center. In April of that year we made the Australian national team at the selection regatta. In May she moved to Penrith so that the two of us could train full-time. Obviously, when training becomes your full-time job, you still have to find a way to make ends meet. One of the local businesses stepped up with a sponsorship proposal that helped. Kathryn also received a disability grant from the Australian Sports Commission, which goes to athletes training for the Paralympic Games. I turned the grant down. Accepting it meant, to me, accepting the label *disabled*. I'm not disabled. Never have been. Never will be.

In August 2007 Kathryn and I headed off to Munich to compete in the World Rowing Championships. Unlike the Paralympic Games, which take place completely apart from the Olympics, the rowing championships were all-inclusive—that is, both para-athletes and conventional athletes were there. I loved it. I sought out the best rowers in the world and peppered them with questions about technique and strategy. By this point I had been rowing for just over six months. I knew I had a lot to learn and not much time to learn it.

Seeking out the best athletes and learning all I can from them has always been my approach, whether it be competing in the Ironman, swimming the channel, or contemplating handcycling around the whole of Australia (which I wisely decided not to do). One of my favorite sayings is "Control the controllables." In other words, focus on what you can do in life, not on what you can't. One of the best ways I've found to do just that is to seek out those who have been there before me and learn everything I possibly can from them. Raw athletic ability will take you only so far, and when it came to rowing, my athleticism didn't exactly fit the sport. Rowing is 70 percent legs, 20 percent lower back, and 10 percent arms. Adaptive rowing Trunk and Arms removes the legs from the equation. The seat doesn't slide, which means there is no push with the legs as in traditional rowing. Just to make sure the legs do not come into play, there is a strap that is secured across the legs just above the knee. Even if my legs had worked, I could not have used them. Instead I had to rely solely upon my lower back and arms. Given the nature of my injuries, my lower back is very weak. Therefore, I needed to learn techniques that would maximize what I could do. I was eager to soak up any advice anyone could give me.

Going into the world championships, Kathryn and I thought the American team would be our toughest competition. They had not lost since the sport was introduced in the para-athlete community. As it turned out, the Americans were not close to us in the finals. However, the Brazil team proved exceptionally strong. Kathryn and I finished second to the Brazilians by a boat length. Our silver medal secured our boat's spot in Beijing. Now we had twelve months to get ready. I set my sights squarely on the Brazilian team. Next time, I vowed, they would not beat us. When we met again in Beijing, I was going to come home with a gold.

A couple of months after the world championships, I was relaxing at home on a warm spring evening. Keep in mind that spring in

Australia is fall in the States. I turned up the music and sank down into my backyard spa, taking in life. Kathryn and I had stepped up our training. My dreams of winning a gold felt very reachable, especially since we had already proven ourselves to be one of the teams to beat the next year in Beijing. I'd dreamed of a gold since the day I won the national 1,500-meter racewalking championships as a twelve-year-old boy. *What better way to end my career,* I said to myself. After Beijing I would be able to tick a gold medal off my list of life's goals and move on to whatever was going to come next

But what is next? I asked myself. *Where do I go from there?* I wasn't thinking in terms of my next athletic challenge or what I might do for a living after retiring as a professional athlete. No, I wondered what was next that would make it worthwhile to get out of bed each morning. My talks with Maurie after my disappointment in the Sydney Games came back to me. *The answers you are looking for aren't going to be found in Hawaii or the English Channel or in the Olympic stadium. You're going to have to find them inside yourself,* he had told me. So what was the answer I was looking for? Maurie had asked me what I most wanted in life. I had answered simply, a family. Seven years later I was still alone.

I looked around my backyard and looked back on my life, at all I had accomplished and all I hoped to do in the future. *So what's missing?* I asked myself. I knew the answer: someone to share this with. *And why is that?* I wondered. I could say I had not met the right person, and perhaps that was true, but I also knew that part of what plagued me when I met with Maurie was still all too present. As long as life was about John Maclean, that's pretty much all I would have in my life: me and more of me. Yes, I had made changes in terms of my life as an athlete. Most of the challenges I had tackled and events I entered focused on raising money and awareness for my foundation, not on gaining glory for myself. At that point in time we had raised and given away over a million dollars to families of children in wheelchairs. I felt confident that I was now making a difference in the lives of others, giving back just as people had given to me right after my accident.

But making a difference in the lives of people I did not know was not enough. With respect to relationships, I had not grown beyond where I was when I met with Maurie. I'd had lots of relationships. But I never really gave myself fully to them. I had still held on to that part of myself Maurie had challenged me to turn loose of. *If things are going to change, I must change first*, I told myself. *If relationships haven't worked, perhaps the problem lies in the way I've approached them, in what I have tried to get out of them.*

Introspection is never an enjoyable experience, especially when one gets completely transparent with oneself. But transparency and honesty are necessary if one is to ever grow. And I was ready to grow. I was ready to change. I was ready to stop living only for myself and find someone with whom I could share life, someone with whom I could be completely myself, and she with me. And when I began to think about who that person might be, there was only one answer.

As I said at the beginning of this chapter, when I met Amanda, it was not love at first sight for either of us. Becoming romantically involved with each other was the furthest thing from either of our minds when we worked together promoting my first book. Over the years the two of us had become dear friends. *Isn't that how it should be?* I asked myself. *Isn't a close friendship the perfect way for a real, lasting relationship to begin?* I knew what I had to do next.

I had a bottle of Dom Pérignon I'd been saving for a special occasion. I called Amanda. "Let's have dinner," I said. Given the state of our schedules, this was not an easy request to work out. However, we managed to find a date that worked for both of us. Amanda agreed to travel out to Penrith and cook dinner if I supplied the wine. She thought this was a simple dinner invitation. She did not yet know I had much longer-range goals in mind.

8

The Quest for Gold

The moment the Beijing Olympic Committee released the image of the gold medal for the upcoming Paralympic Games, I downloaded it onto my computer and printed out four copies. I posted a copy onto my refrigerator and a copy onto the wall facing me in my office. I placed another copy in my gym and the last on my bedroom wall so that it would be the first thing I saw when I woke up.

Throughout my life in sports I have operated by a simple philosophy: See it. Believe it. Achieve it. I didn't post pictures of the gold medal to give myself a goal to aim for. In spite of what my father told me long ago about how it doesn't matter if I win or lose as long as I give it 100 percent, I wasn't going to Beijing to just give it my all and hope for the best. I was going to pick up the gold medal. The way I saw it, and believed it and planned to achieve it, the gold was mine. Any other result simply was not considered.

Of course, being just one of a two-person team, I had to get my partner to think in the same terms. In the months leading up to the games, that's what I set out to do. When we drove in my car to the gym for our afternoon workouts, I cranked up Sting's "Fields of Gold." In the gym I pointed to the picture of the gold medal

I'd posted and I said to Kathryn, "That's ours. Believe it." In one of our rowing sessions at the Sydney Olympic rowing center in Penrith, I stopped the boat in front of the stadium seats and I said to her, "I want you to look up in the stadium. Imagine the stands filled with all our friends and family. See them standing and cheering as we cross the finish line and win the gold." From there we went over to the podium where the medals were awarded in the Sydney Games. "Listen. Do you hear it? That's the sound of our anthem being played as the flag goes up the pole after they place our gold medals around our necks." Kathryn didn't say a word. She just took it all in.

If we had been an ordinary team pushing a slow boat, all the photos of the gold medal and the pep talks on the podium at the Sydney rowing center would have been exercises in futility. But we were not an ordinary team. Our times were fast and getting better. Rowing is a physically punishing sport that taxes every muscle in the body, especially the legs and lower back. In adaptive rowing, the upper body, shoulders, and arms have to make up for what the legs cannot do. That meant spending as much time in the gym as we did on the water. We trained six days a week, sometimes three times a day. On a typical day I was up early, wolfed down breakfast, then arrived at the Penrith Lakes by six. At noon I returned home for lunch, took a one- or two-hour nap, then was back out the door for the gym. In addition to working out, we had a long regimen of recovery exercises.

Strength alone was not enough. Pedro worked with us on strategy as much as technique. We needed his insight because with just over a year of rowing behind me, I did not have a great deal of experience. I listened closely to everything Pedro said. He put together a plan to go out at forty-two strokes a minute for our first ten strokes, then ease back to thirty-six a minute for the rest of the race. We broke the 1,000-meter race into quarters. If we could average 1:02 per 250 meters, we would better Brazil's world-championship winning time by three seconds. Pedro, Kathryn, and I agreed that 4:08 should bring home gold. Because Beijing in September is much warmer and more humid than Sydney, we worked out in the New South Wales Institute of Sport's heat chamber, which we set to eighty-six degrees with 75 percent humidity.

In the midst of all my rigorous training, I was also doing my best to build a new, romantic relationship with Amanda. Things progressed quickly after the weekend where I surprised her with a bottle of Dom Pérignon. Thankfully, our feelings for each other were mutual. From the start, I had only one goal for our relationship: I wanted to marry her and for us to spend the rest of our lives together. However, training six days a week, two and three times a day, left little time for anything else. Through the week, we hardly saw each other. Amanda lived and worked in Sydney, while I lived and trained about an hour away, depending on traffic, in Penrith. On the odd weekday night where I managed to slip into Sydney, I had to get up very early the next morning to make it back to Penrith Lakes to train. On weekends Amanda came out and stayed with me in Penrith.

In spite of the scant amount of time we had together, or perhaps because of it, Amanda and I made the most of what we had. We did not go out at night or socialize with a lot of people. Instead we were happy just to be together and spend time alone. Because of the depth of our friendship, this seemed like a natural next step. We had already gone out in a variety of social settings. Now we were just happy spending quality time together.

The more time we spent together, the more convinced I was that she was *the* one. Some years earlier I had been left a sum of money by my grandparents in Scotland. Rather than take the inheritance in money, I wanted a family keepsake. My uncle Colin was in the jewelry business in Scotland, so I asked him to use my inheritance money to find a beautiful diamond and make me an earring. I thought I would wear it forever as a memento of my grandparents and my Scottish heritage. A few months later a 1.1-carat princess-cut diamond set in platinum arrived at my Penrith home. It was beautiful but far more ostentatious than I had anticipated. I only wore it a couple of times. Now that I found the one with whom I wanted to spend my life, I knew exactly what to do with the diamond.

I managed to get a night away from training in May 2008. Of course, I had to get approval from the coach and do a double session before I left, but it was worth it. Amanda and I went away to the Kings Tableland in the Blue Mountains, one of my favorite places in the world. We managed to get out onto a ledge not far from the parking lot that offered a breathtaking view of the mountains. The two of us sat there, taking it all in, when I turned to Amanda and said, "They say you know when you know, and I know. Will you marry me?"

Without hesitating Amanda said yes, and I opened the jewelry box that contained my family diamond made into a beautiful ring. Tears filled her eyes and mine. Afterward we drove over to a resort in Katoomba where I'd booked a suite. A chilled bottle of Dom Pérignon waited for us in our room. It was a magical night away. At long last I'd found the one, and I planned to never, ever, let her get away. We started making wedding plans and set the date for January 2009. I planned to go to Beijing, pick up my gold, then return to Australia and start working on having a gold-medal marriage.

Unfortunately, romance had to take a backseat to the harsh realities of training at an elite level. Maurie told me years earlier that my life could not revolve around John Maclean, and I took his words to heart. Unfortunately, in the quest for gold, my life did have to revolve around the goal I was chasing. I could not split my time evenly between training and Amanda or anything else. Even taking one day or night off could add tenths of a second to our time in Beijing, and the difference between gold, silver, bronze, and not medaling at all can come down to a tenth of a second. That statement may sound a bit extreme, but it is the reality of sports played at an elite level.

Kathryn and I finally left for Beijing on the first of September, five days before the opening ceremony. I did a television interview with the Australian equivalent of *Good Morning America* before getting on the plane. Friends blew up my phone with messages of encouragement. A large contingent of friends and family came to Beijing to support me. Of course, Amanda was there, as were Johnno and his wife, Gail, and David Knight. My brother Don and his wife, Kelly, also flew over from Canada, while my brother Marc and his wife Anne came up from New Zealand. My good friend and mentor, Marc Robinson, and his wife, Lori, flew in from the United States. Not that I could see Marc or Amanda or anyone else. I stayed in the Olympic Village—something I had not done in Sydney. Unlike Sydney, I did not get caught up in all the excitement and pageantry of the games. During the days leading up to our first heat, Kathryn and I trained and went over last-minute strategic planning with Pedro. As I said in the beginning of the chapter, I fully expected to take home the gold medal. This was to be the crowning achievement of my athletic career.

Our journey to gold did not begin the way I had envisioned. We finished second in our heat to China by nearly four seconds. Only the winner went straight to the finals. I always assumed that would be us. If we had won, we would have had a day off before the final. Instead we had to race in the repechage on the second day of competition. We faced off against Great Britain, the United States, Israel, and Canada. The top two boats went on to the finals the next day. In the repechage, Kathryn and I started off strong and continued to pull away throughout the race. We finished eleven seconds ahead of second-place Great Britain to make the finals comfortably. However, rowing hard on what I had counted on as a rest day worried me. We had to face well-rested teams from Brazil and China. China was the wild card. Four months earlier in the world championships, they had not come close to medaling. Now they were the biggest obstacle between us and gold.

On the day of the finals, eighteen months of training and putting everything else in life on hold came down to a little more than four minutes on the water. Over the course of those four minutes either we would secure a place for ourselves as gold-medal winners for life, or all those months of work would be wasted. To me, those were the only two options.

When Kathryn and I climbed into our boat, we could hear our supporters screaming for us. The noise grew in intensity as we paddled to the start line. Up in the stands were sixty local Chinese people I had never met, all decked out in John Maclean T-shirts. They worked for Dimension Data's Shanghai office. I am currently Brand Ambassador for Dimension Data, and at the time of Beijing I was consulting for them, traveling to Dimension Data offices worldwide, speaking to their employees. Seeing their support in Beijing gave me an extra lift. I remember Drew Ginn, one of the accomplished Olympian rowers to whom I went for advice, telling me that when my body started hurting at the 750-meter mark and I wanted to give in to the pain I should instead use the crowd to get me over the finish line. Hearing the chants of "Aussie, Aussie, Aussie, oi, oi, oi!" and nonstop whistling, I now knew what he meant.

We lined up at the start. The siren sounded. Eighteen months of training kicked in. After 250 meters Brazil had an early lead with us in second. At the halfway point China overtook us while Brazil maintained its lead. Kathryn yelled, "Now!" and we kicked into a different gear, increasing our stroke rate to forty-two strokes a minute. Brazil slid behind us. With 250 meters to go China had a clear lead, but we were closing fast. From the corner of my eye I saw us drawing even. I dug deeper and pushed harder than I ever thought possible. My chest and arms burned. The cheers of the crowd pushed me to ignore the pain. I knew the finish line was just up ahead. I threw myself into the last few strokes. A loud beep sounded as we crossed the finish line. The crowd held its breath for a moment, the finish between China and us having been so close. Deep down I already knew the result. Kathryn threw her arm in the air. I slumped down in my seat. Finally it was official. China won the gold by 0.89 seconds. Given how quickly Kathryn and I were gaining on them, another ten meters and we would have won. But the race was 1,000 meters, not 1,010. I gave Kathryn a high five. She was elated.

As the officials hung the silver around my neck I smiled and put on a good front, but inside I wanted to go off and hide. Knowing we were good enough to have won gold, and missing it by 0.89 of a second—that was hard for me to take. Amanda knew exactly what I was thinking and feeling. A television reporter found her in the stands and asked for her reaction to the race. Keep in mind, for most people, medaling in the Olympics or Paralympics is enough. I'm not most people. Amanda, however, put on the brave front. "It's an amazing achievement to get silver. John will be disappointed initially, but with John's nature, he'll realize it's such a great achievement." That's what she said, all the while thinking, *This is not good. This is not good.* And she was right.

I had to rush off for the postrace drug testing, which made avoiding the media right after the race easy to do. Race officials had me give them a urine sample, and then they drew blood. When I came out of the testing room, I was directed to the pressroom to answer questions. Over and over again I simply deferred to Kathryn. She was ecstatic over the silver. I couldn't share her enthusiasm. It wasn't just that I was so invested in the gold. For me, this was the end of the journey. Coming up less than a second short of gold was the last chapter of my career. Kathryn would go on to find another partner and would have another chance for gold in London or Rio. Not me. This was it—my last best shot.

Amanda and I reunited after my media session. I moved my things out of the Olympic Village and went straight with her to her hotel room. We'd already booked one of the hotel ballrooms for a postrace celebration. Now I had no interest in going to a party, but I knew I had no choice. As soon as we walked into the hotel room, I pulled the silver medal out of my pocket and looked at it. "What am I supposed to do with this?" I said with the same tone I might have used for a speeding ticket. I tossed it toward the corner, fully intending to leave it there. At that moment, in the immediate aftermath of the race, the silver embodied my failure.

"Come on, John," Amanda said. "It's a silver medal. That's an amazing achievement. You have to pull it together. This isn't about only you. Kat is over the moon, and everyone has traveled here for you. All our friends and family as well as Kat's friends and family are waiting for you downstairs. You don't have time to be upset over this. You can have your moment to dwell on this, but it's not now. So get it together and let's get downstairs."

I could not argue. I changed my clothes and wheeled around to leave the room. Amanda turned, took one look at me, and said, "You can't come downstairs without it, you know. Everyone expects to see it." I retrieved my medal, slipped it around my neck, and followed Amanda out of the room without saying a word.

Downstairs the party was in full swing when we arrived. Champagne flowed. There were handshakes, hugs, and smiles all around. "Great job, John," one person after another said. Only those closest to me knew how deeply disappointed I truly was. As the evening wore on I relaxed a bit. At one point I had to make a little speech. I grabbed the microphone and thanked everyone for traveling to China to support us. "Kat, you've been a great partner. I couldn't have asked for a better one. You did a great job out there today. I know we both are a little disappointed, but silver is still a great achievement." I didn't mean that last line. Silver meant I had lost the biggest race of my life.

After the party, I went to the room briefly. I tried to leave the medal there once again, but Amanda wouldn't hear of it. Many of our friends wanted to go out and see the city and hit the hot spots. Begrudgingly, I took the silver along. As Amanda and I climbed into a cab downstairs, the cabdriver turned to me and said in broken English, "Paralympian?"

"Yes," I said.

He became quite excited. "Did you win race?" he asked.

"I got silver," I said with all the enthusiasm of a man on his way to the dentist office.

The cabbie was excited enough for both of us. "Show me, show me!" he said. I pulled out the silver medal for him. "Ooohhhhh," he said with reverence and awe. From that moment on he treated me like royalty. I received the same attention in all the restaurants and bars we visited over the next several days. People recognized the silver medal as an enormous achievement, and for those few days at least, I became quite comfortable with it.

However, when it was time to leave Beijing and fly home, my

disappointment of failing to reach my goal returned. The medal was locked up in the hotel room safe, and I thought about leaving it there. "What am I going to do with it now?" I said to Amanda. "It's not why I came and competed. Why take it home?"

"You're not leaving it here," Amanda replied. "If we have children someday, they will want to see it. It's a part of your legacy. Or, if you really decide in the next few months that you don't want it, we can have it framed with a photo and give it to the staff at North Shore Hospital to inspire others in the spinal unit. Everyone sees this as an amazing achievement. I know you're disappointed, but you'll be more disappointed down the track if you throw it away now."

"But..." I said.

"We're taking it home," Amanda said.

And we did.

I did get my gold from China, however. On our way home we stopped in Shanghai, where we picked out my wedding ring—a gold one. I still have the silver medal. It sits in a safe in our home. The silver and I have grown on each other. I've enjoyed several moments at schools and conferences handing around the medal for others to look at. Today I can clearly see now the achievement that medal represents and the value of having it in years to come. Would I rather it be gold? Go find the quarterback of any team that lost a Super Bowl and ask if he'd rather have won. You'll get the same answer.

9

Tipping Point

Whatever residual disappointment I carried over Beijing completely evaporated on the seventeenth of January 2009 as Amanda walked down a path toward me with her father. A tartan-kilted piper played "Amazing Grace" in the background. I could not believe my good fortune that this woman had agreed to marry me. Her ankle-length, gold-sequined dress shimmered. *This is the gold I've been waiting forty-two years for*, I thought as I watched her come closer to me. We grasped each other's hands when she reached me. There wasn't a dry eye in the place as a solo vocalist sang the Maori love song "Pokarekare Ana." (The Maori are the indigenous people of New Zealand, where Amanda grew up.) The two of us exchanged vows we had written ourselves. A wave of pure joy swept over me when the celebrant said, "I now pronounce you man and wife." For the first time in my life I felt complete, whole. Afterward, during the reception celebration, my father sang "For Once in My Life." Johnno, David Knight, and Amanda's brother Calvin offered speeches. Finally, Amanda and I took a spin around the dance floor, our first as husband and wife.

In the months leading up to Beijing Amanda and I had precious little time together. Between my rigorous training schedule and competition, we grabbed moments here and there as best we could. We made up for lost time after our wedding. Two thousand nine was essentially a yearlong honeymoon. The two of us traveled all over the world because of her work or mine. Although I was not actively competing in anything through the first several months of the year, I spoke at events around the world, thanks in large part to my work with Dimension Data. Amanda's employers, Murdoch Books, kept her busy with travel as well. I can honestly say that this was the first year of my life where my heart and mind were totally and completely focused on enjoying life rather than working toward the next big goal. Those months were a bit like a fairy tale. The culmination of it all came in Las Vegas. Right from the beginning we knew we wanted to have a family, but we also knew we were late starters. We had hoped to become pregnant before the end of the year, and it was now late October. However, on our last big trip of the year to Vegas, we decided to quit worrying about conception and focus instead on enjoying each other. Not long after we returned home we discovered Amanda was indeed pregnant with our son, Jack.

When we returned to Australia in late 2009, life finally felt complete. I had the gold-medal marriage I had dreamed about. To have a son on the way made life all the sweeter. It was a time of transition. I started speaking as often as I could. It soon became the primary source of income I produced for the family.

I also started competing again, but not in rowing. Seven weeks after we returned to Australia I entered the SunSmart Ironman triathlon in Busselton in Western Australia with John Young. Even though Johnno had supported me in my three Hawaiian Ironmans, along with other qualifying events through the years, he'd never competed in an Ironman-length triathlon himself. I told him that the day he finally entered one, I would be right there with him. I kept my word even though I was not physically prepared to compete. In the months before the SunSmart triathlon, I planned on training, but I never got around to it. It's hard to think about triathlon training while traveling the world with your new wife. I didn't worry much about the swim. As I wrote earlier, once you've swum the English Channel, an Ironman swim is not so daunting. The bike portion, however, was another story. I ran out of gas about a third of the way through the 112-mile course. Quitting was not an option. Instead I pulled over to the side of the road and lay down on people's lawns, trying to recover enough to keep going. More than one compassionate soul came out and gave me water and salt to try to fix my cramps. Johnno flew past me. I kept going and finally got to the marathon. That's when I started flying past all those who had passed me earlier, including Johnno. I did not finish before him, though. Instead I waited for him at the finisher's chute for nearly an hour. We went across the line together. It was a special moment.

Not long after the SunSmart triathlon I returned to Hawaii with my friend Matt Beals to compete in the Outrigger Canoe World Championships. We paddled across open ocean in the Kaiwi Channel from Molokai to Oahu, taking first in the 2010 OC2 (ocean canoe, two men) championship. Unlike rowing, paddling had always been a love of mine. If paddling had been a Paralympic sport at the time, I would have competed in that rather than rowing.

With the Molokai challenge behind me, I settled into life as a husband and expectant father. Amanda and I had our Penrith house remodeled, transforming it from the bachelor pad it had been for over two decades into a home fit for a family. She continued commuting back and forth to work in Sydney while I oversaw the remodeling work. Jack was due to arrive soon. I could not wait to become a father.

Around this time I happened to run into a man named Chad King, who was the head coach for the Great Britain adaptive rowing team for Beijing. He dispensed of any small talk and got straight to the point: "I watched you row in Beijing," he said. "You should have won the gold. If you are interested, I think I can help you win gold in London."

My first reaction was to say, "Thanks, but I am retired." I didn't. I thanked Chad and said, "Let me give that some thought." As I've said before, I have always believed there is no such thing as a coincidence. Even before my accident, people have entered my life at just the right moment in a way that cannot be pure chance. If I had not been demoted from the Penrith Panthers and moved on to Warragamba, I never would have met John Young. Without him, I might have forever sunk into a sea of despair and pity in the hospital following my accident. I surely never would have competed in my first Nepean Triathlon, which led to everything else I accomplished in my life in sports. David Knight also entered my life at the very moment I needed him most, even though I did not know it at the time. Without him, I never would have crossed the English Channel, nor he without me. And then there is Amanda. Not only would she not normally have been assigned to work with me in promoting my first book, but the timing of my asking her to move our relationship beyond friendship could not have been coincidental. No, I do not believe in coincidences. When a "chance" meeting with someone like Chad King occurs, I take it very, very seriously.

Fast-forward a few months. Jack arrived two weeks after we finished the remodel on our house. Amanda and I were over the moon. Because we both waited longer than most to settle down and get married, we were older than most first-time parents. I think that only made both of us appreciate our experience that much more. We had the typical sleepless nights and everything that comes with a new baby, but we tried to relish the experience as much as we could. Honestly, I hadn't known if I would ever have the privilege of becoming a dad, and I didn't know if it would happen again.

In the midst of all of this, another "coincidence" occurred. Kathryn came by to see me. After I retired from rowing, she found a new partner and kept on competing. She and her new partner had recently competed at the world championships and hadn't done well. "I can only win gold with you, John, so I need you to make a comeback," she said.

"That's all well and good," I said, "but I already put a lot of time and energy into that goal and we didn't get it. I'm married now and I have a family, and they are where I'm putting all my time and energy these days."

Kathryn was not inclined to take no for an answer. Apparently my taking her onto the medal stand and asking her to imagine winning the gold had sunk in. When we first met, she saw herself the way she had been as a girl, as the last person chosen for the team. Now she clearly saw herself as an elite athlete capable of winning her sport's biggest prize. "I appreciate that, John, I really do, but I also know this: We very nearly won the gold in Beijing and probably should have. I'm a better rower now than I was then. But if I'm going to get better, then I better make sure my partner is the best I can get."

She sounded like me a couple of years earlier. Clearly, Kathryn had reached the point where she wouldn't raise her fist in triumph over a silver. That piqued my interest. My earlier conversation with Chad replayed in my mind. What were the odds that I would just happen to run into him? And now Kathryn was here, talking to me about making a comeback. I had to consider it. "Let me talk to Amanda," I said.

Later that evening I approached Amanda with the idea. Both of us knew full well the sacrifices we'd made leading up to Beijing. Even though we were engaged then, sacrificing time with each other was not as difficult then as it would be now. Before, it was just the two of us. Amanda was busy with work and often away. However, now there were three of us. I wouldn't just lose time with my wife. I would also lose time with my newborn son. It was a high price to pay. I told Amanda, "I know it is a lot, but I feel it is something I should seriously consider. I hate going out with silver when it should have been gold."

Amanda listened thoughtfully. "How will your training schedule work? I've got Jack in day care and work in the city. I need some help managing if you've got a full training schedule."

"I'll need to spend most of the week in Canberra at the Institute of Sport training facilities," I said.

"Seriously? Just home at weekends?" She paused for a moment. "I have to think this through. I'm going for a walk."

Quite a bit of time passed. Jack and I hung out together, waiting. Finally, when Amanda returned, she said, "Okay. I married you understanding what drives you. I don't want you to have any regrets. Go and win the gold medal, and we'll 'get the band back together' for London. We'll take Jack, and he can look back in years to come at photos of the two of you with the gold around your neck and see that he was a part of your last amazing achievement. It will be a moment the two of you will share for the rest of your lives."

The sacrifices we knew we were making went beyond the time I would be away from Amanda and Jack. We had given some consideration to having a second child. Given our ages (Amanda was forty when Jack was born, and I was forty-four), we knew we would need to plan for a second in the short term, and that in itself was somewhat daunting with Amanda working and Jack just a year old. However, the moment we decided I would throw myself into going for gold, we both knew that meant Jack would be an only child. Amanda could not juggle work an hour from home with both a toddler and a new baby while I lived three hours away, only coming home on weekends. But we were blessed with our little man, and we were happy to be just the three of us.

That's how, with my wife's blessing, I came out of retirement and threw myself back into a quest for a gold medal. I shuttled between Canberra and home while Amanda bore the brunt of my decision. She woke up early, got Jack ready for day care and herself for work. Then it was out the door for the hour-long commute to Sydney, which many days stretched to an hour and a half because of traffic. After work she drove another hour home, picked Jack up, played out the evening routine, then got up the next morning to do it all again. I tried to work out a compromise with the Paralympic governing body and spend four days in Canberra, then rush home for three with the family.

Kathryn and I only had a few months to get back up to speed before the 2011 world championships. We took the bronze, which we both considered a good start, given we'd only been back in the boat together a couple of months. More than that, we qualified our boat for London. Now we had a little less than a year to get ready for another run at gold. When I say we qualified the boat, that's exactly what I mean. A boat from Australia was assured a spot in the 2012 Paralympic Games because of our result at the world championships. While one would assume that meant Kathryn and I would be in the boat, that was not guaranteed. Of course, at the time this little detail felt like nothing more than a technicality. After all, we were the silver medalists from Beijing and actually the only two adaptive rowers in the category in Australia, or so I thought.

Not long after Kathryn and I qualified the boat, the governing body, Rowing Australia, reclassified another Paralympic rower into the Trunk and Arms category. He had been rowing in the Legs, Trunk, and Arms category, and his reclassification now placed him in a position to challenge to be Kathryn's partner. The difference is this: Legs, Trunk, and Arms includes rowers with a vision impairment or physical impairment, including cerebral palsy or acquired brain injury, limb loss or deficiency, nerve damage, or other similar impairment. Rowers are able to use a sliding seat and use their legs, trunk, and arms to perform the stroke. Trunk and Arms rowers have no or limited use of their legs and therefore do not use a sliding seat to perform their stroke. Gavin, the reclassified rower, had reasonable use of his legs, which is why he was in the former category. However, the governing body determined his use was now limited enough that he should be moved into our class. All of this meant that suddenly my spot in the boat was no longer a sure thing. I had to win it over the course of the upcoming season.

You might wonder why the powers that be didn't simply put together a second mixed team and create a more competitive training environment. That simply was not an option, because there were no female candidates for a second team. Paralympics draw from a small pool of athletes, and there are generally several categories in each sport to allow for differences in individual athletes' mobility. In spite of its large landmass, Australia is a relatively small country population-wise. In practical terms, this meant that Gavin and I split time in the boat with Kathryn. Gavin also moved to Canberra full-time, while I continued going home to my family as often as I could get away.

None of this worried me. I never for a moment doubted that Kathryn and I would represent Australia in London in 2012.

Unlike previous athletic quests, I wasn't doing this for John Maclean. This was a family effort. This was for all three of us, and that's how I approached it. We all made the sacrifices, and I refused to let those sacrifices be for nothing. Even Gavin's emergence as a rival did not deter me. Competition is healthy. With him pushing me, my best would surely come out.

However, life doesn't always follow our best-laid plans. Chad had replaced Pedro as our coach. Even though he was the one who pulled me out of retirement, he made no guarantees as London drew close. Right before the final qualifying competition for London, he came to me and said, "The committee will make a decision on who is in the boat based on performances in the last race in Italy."

"Okay," I said, undeterred. All of my friends and family had already started making plans to travel to London. Some had booked their flights and secured hotel rooms. Not making the team was a consideration I never let reach my conscious thought.

"The committee is going to give the first opportunity to race to Gavin," Chad added. The upcoming regatta included both singles and doubles competition, each taking place over the course of the weekend. Our boat was scheduled to run on back-to-back days. This meant Gavin would row with Kathryn on the first day, when both were fresh. I would row the second day.

"Why?" I asked. "Kathryn and I won silver in Beijing. We qualified the boat for London. We've been a successful team for some time now. Shouldn't I have the first crack at keeping my place in the boat?"

"You rowed first in the last race," Chad replied.

"Well, at least you will have the Biomec data in the boat to compare our stroke rates and the force of each," I countered. Biomec is a piece of equipment that goes on the gate of the boat where the oar attaches. It measures the output of each stroke.

"We didn't bring it this time," Chad said. "We will just go by the race results."

"But Kathryn will obviously be more fatigued on the second day. How can you compare the results between the two days?"

"That's the criteria the committee decided on," Chad replied, ending the conversation.

As one might expect, the boat went faster on the first day than the second. Halfway through the course I felt the boat get heavy, which means I felt Kathryn's strength start to give from the fatigue of rowing hard on back-to-back days. Even so, both Gavin and I competed in the individual events, where I had the better time by fifteen seconds.

Soon after returning to Australia, my phone rang. It was the head selection coach. "We've decided to go with Gavin."

"What? Why?" I couldn't believe my ears. "What is the justification for making a change on a winning team?"

He answered my question but not in a way that made any sense to me. I countered every argument he gave. All he could say in return was, "You can take it up with the appeals committee."

When we hung up, I took a deep breath, tried to steady myself, and made another call. Amanda answered. "Hey" she said, anxious. She knew why I was calling.

"No," was all I could say.

Amanda let out a long sigh. Finally she said, "What's the story?"

No was the only word I could muster up. I didn't know what else to say. All the months and months of sacrifice—for what? I had missed my son's first steps because I was away in Canberra. *His first steps!* I could not put into words what I felt in that moment. I wished Kathryn had let me be. I wished I had never run into Chad and let him plant the idea of coming back in my head. Everything happens for a reason, I've always told myself. Nothing happens by chance. But I could not see the reason in this.

Normally I would have spent a few days or a few weeks stewing over the disappointment; then I would lift myself up and move on. Since my days in the hospital after my accident, I have refused to wallow in self-pity. After my disappointment and embarrassment in the Sydney Games, it took spending time with Maurie to get me back up and going again, but eventually I got there. I wanted to do the same thing now. I wanted to put this behind me as far and as fast as possible.

There was only one problem. I had to call my friends and family who had already booked their flights to London. I had to personally tell them that they could still go to the Paralympic Games, but I would not be there. The calls were never short. Every conversation turned into me recounting the story in much greater detail than I did in this chapter. Everyone had the same reaction: "This isn't right, John...You've been robbed...Can't you do something?" All were outraged, and their anger just pulled me right back to the moment when I first got the call telling me I had lost my place in the boat.

Even after all the phone calls were made, I could not get away from the disappointment. People came up to me in Penrith and said, "I heard you came out of retirement. When do you leave for London?" I tried to give a brief answer, but it always elicited more questions and always led to the same reaction: "This isn't right, John...You've been robbed...Can't you do something?"

Amanda was eager for us to get on with life. In the months after we finished the remodel on my house in Penrith, the two of us began discussing moving to Sydney. Her hour-long commute had long since grown wearisome. Increasingly, my speaking engagements took me back into the city. Living so far away didn't make a great deal of practical sense. On top of that, the Penrith house had been my house. I bought it with money I received as part of the settlement with the trucking company after my accident. Both of us thought it would be advantageous to find a house that could be ours. Now that I wasn't going to London, there seemed to be no reason to delay moving forward with these plans. However, every time Amanda tried to bring up the subject, I simply wasn't ready. I could not get over the disappointment of being dropped from the London team. Every time I tried, another conversation sucked me right back into it.

Finally, Amanda reached the end of her patience. She had given me as much time as she could to get over this on my own, but now the aftermath of not making London was even more intrusive than the original training schedule had been. Thankfully, she didn't just tell me to suck it up and get over it. Instead, she gave me a gift of a week away to a health retreat for my birthday. "Go. Clear your mind," she said. "And when you come back, come back. I need you here with me—all of you: body, mind, and spirit."

I went away for five days. In those five days I could clearly see that all that had just transpired was not wasted time. I returned home with a new goal, one I would not rest until I reached: I was going to walk again.

10

Where Is the Door Marked "Walking"?

All my life I have lived by the simple philosophy that when one door closes, another will open. Finding it is simply a matter of stilling oneself and becoming open to the possibilities the new door presents. Then, when the new possibility opens up, you must pursue it with all you have. I always hearken back to my father's words when I was just a boy. "John," he told me, "it doesn't matter if you win or lose, just as long as you give it one hundred percent." I have always tried to do just that, whether it was running about the football fields as a young man or pushing myself through the punishing lava fields of Kona in the Ironman or coming up 0.89 seconds short of a gold medal in Beijing. In everything I have done I have given my all, holding nothing back.

When I went away to the health retreat following the disappointment of London, I discovered the next challenge to which I would give my 100 percent. I should say "rediscovered," for finding this challenge was really nothing more than coming to the realization that the dream I had harbored since the day the truck hit me on the M4 had never really gone away. All my athletic pursuits, from my first triathlon in a wheelchair to trying to make the 2012 London Paralympic team, were really attempts to fill the void the disappointment of never reaching this dream created. But the desire never went away. All along I freely admitted that I would trade everything to be able one day to walk and run again. Twenty-five years earlier I thought I had settled the issue, and perhaps I had. But no more. I wanted to walk, and during my week at the health retreat I made up my mind that that was exactly what I was going to do.

I didn't know that's where the week at the retreat was going to lead when I wheeled through the front door. I arrived there determined to get back to a good place where I could once again fully engage with my family. As I did after returning from Beijing, I planned on finding a way to build my speaking business when I got home. My motivational speaking engagements had slowed even before I threw myself back into training for the 2012 games. I expected them to pick up once again when I came back from London with a gold medal. Obviously, that was not going to happen now. But I thought I could improve as a speaker and build this into a viable business. To motivate others, I had to get myself out of this funk I was in, and that was why I went off to the health retreat.

On my next-to-last day at the retreat center, I made an appointment with a hypnotherapist named Sonja. I went into her office with feelings of anxiety and tension. Constantly reliving the experience of being dropped from the boat for London through having to tell the story time after time after time had taken its toll. With the games only a few weeks away, I feared the worst was in front of me. That's why I was here to see Sonja. I needed a way to cut through the stress and start moving forward again.

Sonja quickly put me at ease. "This isn't like some carnival sideshow, John. You will not be completely under in our session. You'll always stay aware of where you are and in control of yourself."

"Okay," I said.

"I want you to sit back and relax completely. I need you to concentrate on your breathing. Turn loose of any thoughts you're holding on to. You are in a safe place. Relax and just be."

Surprisingly, I found I was able to follow Sonja's instructions very easily. A few weeks earlier I had begun experimenting with deep meditation, which involved many of the same techniques. My body relaxed, my mind emptied of all the thoughts thrashing about, and I was able to be fully in the moment with her and nowhere else.

With me in this completely relaxed state, Sonja asked a few guided questions directed to my higher self. The question that I remember most vividly was simply, "John, what do you want to do?"

"I want to walk and I want to run," I answered. The words sort of surprised me as they came out.

"How do you see that happening?" she asked.

"I don't know," I said.

More conversation followed until Sonja said, "Now I want to go back, back before the accident, back to when you were a young man. Think about what you were doing then." She paused to let me travel there in my mind. After a few questions to this part of myself, she asked, "What is it that you aspire to?"

"I want to walk and I want to run."

She followed that up with a few more questions before taking me even further back in my mind to my fourteen-year-old self. Again, she asked the same question, and again, I gave the same answer. But, as always, I did not know how I could make this happen. I only knew it was what I most wanted out of life now.

As our session came to a close, Sonja said, "To me, it seems your life is focused on one purpose: walking again. However, reaching this purpose is going to be very different from everything you've done before. In sport, you decided on an event and you knew when it would take place. You had some control over it as well as control over how you prepared and pushed yourself to get there. This is very different. You are not in control. This will unfold when it is meant to unfold. You need to step away, because you cannot control what reaching this goal is going to look like. You don't know how to get there, so you need to relax and let it happen as it happens."

I immediately bought into the idea of focusing on the singular purpose of walking again. However, Sonja's words to relax and let it happen as it happens left me perplexed. With every sport challenge, I always tried to control the controllable as I worked toward my goal. Now she was telling me my entire goal fell into the realm of the uncontrollable. How, then, was I supposed to get there?

I ran into Sonja the next morning before leaving for home. "I had a dream about you last night, John," she said, very excited. "In my dream you were standing onstage and were so full of life and energy. I've never had that experience before."

"That's lovely," I said, but in the back of my mind I was thinking, *Let's try and see how far we can go with this whole idea of walking.* I then wheeled out the door and toward my car, just as I had wheeled in five days earlier.

Letting things happen as they happen is not how I've ever done anything. When I returned home to Penrith, I told Amanda what had happened. "So what does this mean?" she asked.

"I'm not sure," I replied, "but I am going to find out."

"What about the house? Are you ready to make a decision on selling the house and moving closer to Sydney?"

"I don't know," I said, which probably was not the best answer. Honestly, I had not given the house a thought while I was away. Now I guess I had no choice. We talked further about moving. Over the next several weeks we reached a decision to put the house on the market. Again, that's not really where my head was. I wanted to walk, and I had a hard time thinking about anything else.

Over the next few months I applied what I had learned about meditation to my quest. The friend who opened my eyes to meditation explained that we can actually create things for ourselves through first visualizing them. To me, this sounded very much like my approach to sports: See it. Believe it. Achieve it. I meditated every day, often twice a day, for forty-five minutes at a time. It was amazing. As I went deeper into a meditative state, I not only saw myself running, but I felt the ground beneath my feet and the wind blowing through my hair. With time, I found I could so relax my body that an outside observer might call 911 in fear that I had slipped into a coma. I focused on creating the reality I hoped to achieve. *See it. Believe it. Achieve it.* I could see it. I believed it. Achieving was only a matter of time.

I told Amanda about my sessions when she returned home from work. Ever practical, she didn't get caught up in my enthusiasm. "I think it's great; I think the visualization and mental agility you're developing is awesome," Amanda said more than once, "but I think there are limits to how far it can take you. I don't think you will just get up from a session one day and take off walking. I just don't. I'm sorry. Do you?"

I didn't know. I had no idea how I would walk again, but I was convinced I would. I simply had to get my mind in a state where it could perceive the signs that it was time to take that first step. Over the last several months of 2012 I became very in tune with my body. Every muscle twitch in my legs caused me to wonder, Could this be the start?

"I'm not sure how it will happen," I replied to Amanda, "but I do believe I can have a part in creating the reality I hope to see happen."

Ever the pragmatist, Amanda said, "Sure, I just think there are limits to what you can do on your own, John. I think you may walk again, but I think it will come through some new medical breakthrough—maybe something like stem cells, or the next breakthrough to come."

The two of us had variations of this same conversation for months. In the midst of all this I went to see my regular physical therapist, Rob. Over the years Rob had pushed and pulled and stretched my muscles and limbs back into working shape time and time again. Since 1995 I'd had chronic shoulder problems that Rob regularly took care of. I went to see him not long after my session with Sonja the hypnotherapist, but not for my shoulder. Cutting right to the chase I said to him, "Rob, I want to walk again. Can you help me?" My voice cracked as the last sentence came out.

Rob looked at me, silent. His eyes misted. He swallowed hard. I could tell he didn't know what to say.

"I don't mean I expect you to get me up and walking again," I said. "I believe I will walk again. How it will happen is anyone's guess, but I know it will. I would like for you to help me do some things that might put me in a better position to act when the opportunity presents itself."

"I can do that," Rob said with an uncertain tone in his voice. "Let's get you standing up and see what we've got." I had always been able to stand for short bursts of time. To stand for any time at all, I had to lean up against something. Rob stood me up and went to work on my posture. "Imagine you have a string pulling you up straight through the top of your head," he told me. Again, I didn't expect him to have some new treatment that might lead me to take a step. I'd been through all sorts of PT over the previous twenty-five years. I knew what to expect. This wasn't about taking my first steps but about being ready for when that time came.

Throughout the last few months of 2012 I went deeper and deeper into my meditation. Amanda's company sold. By Christmas we knew her work with them would soon end. Choosing to see this as an opportunity rather than a problem, we made plans to see more of the world as a family. With our house now up for sale, we decided to spend three months in Hawaii during 2013. Both of us love the islands, and we couldn't think of a better place to go and regroup as we tried to figure out where life might take us next. We went to Oahu for a couple of weeks before the end of the year to find a rental house. While we were there I met more people who confirmed I was on the right track in my meditation efforts with an eye toward regaining use of my legs.

Athletically, this was a very dry season for me. For the first time since before I completed my first triathlon as a wheelie, I didn't know what to do next. The London Games had come and gone. Kathryn and her new partner did not medal, but that did not make me want to go back into that sport and give it another go for Rio in 2016. I was never overly passionate about rowing. I could do it, and I thought I was relatively good at it, but I did not miss it.

In early January 2013, I received a phone call from a friend with the Paralympics. "Great news, John," he said. "Paddling has been added for Rio, both kayak and Va'a." Va'a, or V-1, is a one-person outrigger canoe very similar to those I paddled in the Molokai challenges I completed.

"That is great news. What do I need to do if I want to explore this further?" I replied. I love paddling, a sport very different from rowing. I've loved it since Johnno and I bought a kayak together and paddled it up and down the Nepean River in 1990. This was my first love, at least for sports on the water.

"Go over to the lakes at Penrith. We'll get you going there."

I borrowed a boat and paddle and headed over to the lakes the following week. Two weeks later I had an opportunity to race at the state championships. I had entered just to set a benchmark for myself, to see where I stood with zero training. The results were encouraging. My time in the final was just over a second slower than the current Australian champion. I'd found my next big thing.

Immediately, I set my sights on Rio. Our dream for London where I would win the gold, hoist Jack onto my lap, and snap a photograph that would hang on his wall was simply pushed back four years to Rio 2016. My days of deep meditation became days of training and paddling down at the lakes. I spent three or four days a week there, and my times showed it. Comparing them to the best times in the world, I was right there. With three and a half years to prepare for the Rio games, I believed my dream of a gold medal was very, very attainable. I started looking about for the best boat and equipment. At this point I was still using borrowed equipment at the rowing center at the lakes. I had my new goal. All of my focus was now on paddling and Rio.

However, as I trained I ran into an old problem. I had hurt my left shoulder in the 1995 Hawaiian Ironman, and it had never been quite the same since. Massages and physical therapy had been part of my training routine ever since. Once I started paddling again I had to go see Rob about once a week for him to ease my shoulder pain. Amanda had learned how to help the pain as well, which she had to do in between my visits with Rob. My shoulder problem was more than an annoyance. The shoulder seemed to be getting worse, not better. Both Amanda and I feared that I might need surgery on it in the not-too-distant future. I don't have to say how inconvenient that would be for me as a wheelie, or for us as a family. You can't push yourself in a chair with one arm, not without going around and around in circles.

The growing pain in my shoulder added to the regular pain I had lived with since the day of my accident. Because I am an incomplete paraplegic, my accident left me hypersensitive to pain. Even though I have not mentioned this fact since the first chapter, the hypersensitivity never went away. My bum hurt if I sit too long (i.e., in a wheelchair). Most nights I woke up with pain in my right foot. Because I lack hip abductor muscles, I could pull my knee right up to my chest and hold my foot tucked just under my ribs. Many nights that is how I would drift off to sleep, holding my foot tucked into my body, massaging it over and over, trying to quell the pain. I also lived with stiffness in my back. All of it I simply learned to live with. I think for years I overcame my day-to-day discomfort with the pain we thrive on as athletes. I was burning up my arms and upper body so much doing Ironman and swimming, day-to-day pain just seemed part of the journey. However, the growing problems with my shoulder had me and my wife concerned.

Amanda, Jack, and I took off for a getaway up in Queensland in northern Australia, where it is quite warm. In the land Down Under, it gets colder as you go south and warmer as you go north. The three of us were having a great break away as a family, and catching up with friends we don't see often. One of those friends was Pete Jacobs. Pete is one of the premier triathletes in the world and an ambassador for the John Maclean Foundation. He won the Hawaiian Ironman world championship in Kona in 2012 after finishing second there in 2011. I knew Pete had been battling a couple of injuries, but when I saw him, he appeared to be pain-free.

"I found an interesting new therapist," Pete explained to me, "a guy up north named Ken Ware. Let me tell you, mate, the guy is amazing. I went in to see him limping and came out sprinting. It's pretty unconventional. I've definitely never done anything like it, but I bet he could help with your shoulder."

Amanda and I looked at each other. "Sounds like it is worth a try," Amanda said. "Why don't you give him a call?"

11

Three Small Steps

My forearms started shaking. The tremor spread up my arms and across my shoulders. My arms rocked back and forth in perfect rhythm with one another. I struggled to hold on to the handles of the chest-press machine. As the tremor grew in intensity, my hands whipped the handles back and forth. The main pulley that connected the handles to the weights banged against the metal frame of the machine. In spite of the loud clanging, I kept my eyes closed, cleared my mind, and allowed my body to accept the current that was flowing through it.

The spasm spread down my shoulders, causing my body to wobble from side to side as if an earthquake was rolling beneath me. I felt Ken Ware's light touch on my back, keeping me in place. "Let it evolve," he said. "Don't try to resist it." The shaking grew in intensity. Before I knew what was happening my legs began to jump and jerk in and out as I straddled the chest-press machine. The movement in my legs really caught me by surprise. As the tremor evolved, both the left and right leg mirrored one another, moving in and out, in and out in unison as the rest of my body rocked about like I'd been jolted with electricity. The machine clanged. My hands could barely hold on to the handles, much less keep the little bit of weight on the machine in place. "That's good. That's good," Ken repeated.

My eyes closed, entire body shaking, the tremor kept going and going. I'd never experienced anything like it, and I'd spent most of my adult life on weight machines in the gym. "Keep your eyes closed. I need you to try to stand outside yourself and just observe what is happening," Ken Ware said. "Don't react to it, or try and stop it. Just let it go."

I nodded my head, although I'm not sure if Ken could tell that's what I was trying to do. My head rocked with the tremor that had overtaken my body. I held my grip on the chest-press handles and tried to continue moving them slowly, methodically forward and back just as Ken had instructed me. By this point, slow and methodical looked more like a frog in a sock.

"Good. Good," Ken said with a soft, reassuring tone. "Be the observer. Let it go and don't attach yourself to the process of what's happening right now."

The velocity of the tremor increased. My body felt like it could slip off the machine at any moment. I strained to keep my eyes closed, to let the tremor sweep over me without reacting to it. My months of meditation paid off as I took control over my breathing and turned off the torrent of random thoughts running through my mind. *Take it in. Observe. Listen to what your body is telling you*, I told myself. I felt like an earthquake fault had opened up inside me.

Then, after what seemed like a very long time but was in truth just a few moments, the tremor began to subside. My legs slowed to a stop. My shoulders stopped shaking. Finally, my arms and hands grew still. I lowered the weight and stopped.

"Okay, you can open your eyes," Ken said to me.

"Wow! What was that?" I asked.

Ken smiled. "Your nervous system is starting to recalibrate itself, turning loose all the stored emotion you've packed in over the past forty-seven years. All that emotion acts like an internal brake inside of you. It's what holds you back and inhibits you from letting your body do what it is capable of doing."

"And I thought I was here to have you take a look at my sore shoulder," I said with a laugh.

"Everything is connected, John. Your mind and body and emotions, your past, present, and future—they're all intertwined. We're focusing on your whole system, not a specific injury. We're fixing the connections and essentially rebooting your system by setting free the stored-up, internal chaos."

"Why didn't a tremor come about on the first couple machines you put me on?" I asked. When the tremor began, Ken and I had been at it for over an hour, moving slowly from one weight machine to another with a series of exercises, all of which used low resistance and very slow repetitions.

"I would say, John, the truly remarkable thing is that the tremors began on this first day after only an hour. That's quite unusual. Many times it takes longer for someone to silence the noise in their brains and let the natural chaotic rhythms of their nervous system take over," Ken replied.

"I've spent a lot of time in meditation," I replied.

"It shows," he said.

Even though Ken and I had known each other for all of twenty-four hours, I had already begun to build a level of trust with him. We hit it off from the moment he picked me up at the airport when I flew up from Sydney to his center in Emerald in northeastern Australia. (That's about the same distance as New York to St. Louis.) For the past twenty-five years Ken had been practicing his theory, tapping into the nervous system, but he was also a body builder and a runner. That created some common ground between us. Through the years, he'd done a great deal of research into the ways in which the laws of physics and biology interact within the human body, all of which builds on chaos theory. Ken works with some impressive people in the scientific community all around the world, and his work has been published in prestigious science journals. On top of that, I kept going back to what my friend Pete had said—that he came to Ken limping and left sprinting. Science is all well and good, but results really grab my attention.

"Take a seat on the lateral pull-down," Ken said.

I shifted over from the chest-press machine into my wheelchair and wheeled across Ken's gym to the lat pull-down. As a wheelchair athlete, I spent a lot of time over the years building my upper-body muscles, so this was familiar territory. Ken set the weight at ten pounds, the lowest setting on the machine. Obviously, this was not to be a strength-building exercise.

"Close your eyes, John. Switch off the visual cortex so that the two hemispheres of your brain can communicate with one another. I also want you to be fully present with me. Turn off the internal dialogue and stop chasing thousands of random thoughts running about your head. Now, I want you to push out with your arms very slowly and focus on the resistance you feel."

I slowly pushed on the handles. "Equal and even, John. Make sure the force is equal and even," Ken said. "Imagine there's a line cutting right down the middle of your body. Let go and let the two sides communicate."

I did my best to do just that. As I pushed against the resistance on my arms, my eyes closed, I found my anxiety level rising. The weight on the machine was very small, and I'd done literally thousands, if not tens of thousands, of reps on machines just like this, but there was something about pushing this low weight so slowly, with my eyes closed, that made the weight seem suddenly heavy and caused my anxiety to grow.

"Turn off the internal dialogue and let go," Ken said, as if he had a camera inside my mind. "The anxiety you feel is normal. The resistance from the weights brings it up to the surface."

Sitting there, eyes closed, pushing slowly against such light resistance that suddenly felt very, very heavy, my mind raced. I went back to my months of meditation to gain control, which proved far from easy in spite of my success on the previous machine. I felt old emotions flooding up to the surface.

It was as though Ken could read my mind. "Let go of the accident. Let go of the truck. Let go of whoever first told you that you would never walk again."

A thought flashed through my mind. *Who told me I would never walk again?* Names and faces flashed through my mind. The doctors never said it. The therapists didn't. *Who did?* Then I remembered. It was me. No one else had to say it because they knew it to be true. They waited for me to admit it to myself.

It is difficult to describe the sensation I felt as my arms pushed against the ten pounds of resistance, my eyes closed. The closed eyes are the key. I've spent most of my life in gyms. I feel at home there. But pressing against the weight, not doing reps but just feeling the resistance with my eyes closed, trying to keep my mind neutral, I felt very, very vulnerable. And when you feel vulnerable, you want to snap back and try to take control of the situation to make yourself safe. Ken wanted me to do just the opposite. He wanted me to feel the vulnerability and embrace it.

Be present, I reminded myself. *Not in the past. Not in the future. Be here. Now. On this machine. Feel the weight. Embrace this moment.* The tremors quickly followed, once again starting in my arms. The weights bounced. The machine clanged. The tremor evolved throughout my body. Now that I knew what to expect, I found it easier to let it roll. The intensity increased. My legs shook in front of me, this time almost violently. I arched back, eyes closed, breathing slowly. As I relaxed, the intensity increased beyond anything I experienced before. I didn't expect it. "That's how it works," Ken said. "The more relaxed you are and the slower you move the weight, the more chaotic the tremor becomes."

"I guess that means it's working," I said after the tremor had passed.

Ken laughed. "That's right. As you connect with the resistance, the entire nervous system gets involved. We aren't just working one part of your body. The lat pull-down machine wasn't so much working your muscles as it was tapping into your entire nervous system to release the tension you have built up in it, sort of like releasing a wound-up rubber band."

"That makes sense," I said. "What now?"

"That's it for today. We'll do more on the same machines tomorrow, then build from there on the third and fourth days."

Altogether the first session in his gym lasted a little over two and a half hours. By the end of our session the pain in my shoulder and my right leg and bum had greatly diminished. Unfortunately, the reduced pain did not result in better sleep. That night I tossed and turned in bed. At times my body shook like small aftershocks from the tremors that afternoon. When I did manage to get to sleep, I found myself barraged by the most bizarre dreams. It was one of the worst nights of sleep of my life.

The next morning Ken had a sly smile on his face and asked, "How did you sleep?" His tone told me he already knew the answer.

"Awful," I said. "But something tells me you already knew that."

Ken laughed. "That's part of the recalibration process. It is like your nervous system is doing a data dump. You should get back to normal sleep in a day or two."

That day we went through the same series of exercises. The tremors came quicker and stronger. At the end of the session Ken sat down on a bench across from me. "So how do you feel?" he asked.

"Good," I replied. "Really good."

"And the shoulder?"

"Better." I moved my right arm about. "Better than it has in a long time," I said, nodding and smiling.

"Good. Good," Ken said. Then he paused for a moment before saying, "You came here for your shoulder, but I think there's more to it than that. What do you really want to do, John?"

"I want to walk and I want to run," I replied without having to give the question a thought. Even though I had turned my attention to paddling and getting ready for a gold-medal run in Rio, I still wanted to walk as much as I did when I came home from the health retreat several months earlier. Who am I kidding? Even if I had not been to the retreat and hadn't had my session with Sonja, and even if I had not spent months doing deep meditation where I saw myself walking and running again, I would have given Ken the same answer. After twenty-five years in a wheelchair, my dream of walking again had never died.

"Based on the activity I have observed in your legs the past couple of days, I don't see any reason why you shouldn't be able to do that," Ken replied.

I could hardly believe my ears. When I arrived at Ken's house two days before, I had to use my crutches to support my weight and carry me up the steps to his non-wheelchair-friendly house. He walked right beside me. He could see how my legs did not work and yet he believed they could. I was beyond encouraged. It was as though I had arrived here at just the right moment and found just the right person to help me. "Really?" I said.

"Yes. When the tremors began on all the machines, your legs responded in a bilaterally stable manner." He showed me a few video clips. "Watch," Ken said. "Notice how the right leg doesn't lag behind but mirrors the movement of the left. That tells me information is getting through from the brain all the way down to the foot. John, your legs responded to the tremor like someone without a spinal cord injury."

Now he really had my attention. "Really? How is that possible?" I asked.

"Your spinal cord injury is like a roadblock on a highway that keeps the neurons from moving up and down. Because you have pushed yourself physically with all you have done in sport over the past twenty-five years, the neurons have found a way to bypass the roadblock and get through," Ken said.

"And that is why I should be able to walk?"

"Yes. I don't see any reason why you shouldn't be able to," Ken said.

"Okay, let's give it a go. What do I need to do?" I asked.

"We'll start working on your legs more tomorrow."

True to his word, Ken worked on my legs through the second day. And the third. And the fourth. He still used upper-body machines, but he focused more attention on leg exercises, each time watching my legs closely. Or I assume he did. My eyes were closed, after all.

At the end of our session on the fourth day Ken said to me, "Let's stand up…If you want to start to walk, you've got to put your right foot on the ground—that is, you've got to give it information of what you want it to do."

I had tried to take steps in the past, and when I did, I ran into two problems. First, I cannot move my right foot up and down. Medically this is known as foot drop. When I try to move my leg, the foot drags below and makes me fall right over. For that reason, whenever I hobble about with my crutches, I put all of my weight on my arms and keep balance and direction with my left leg while protecting my right by tucking it up off the ground behind my left. I protect it because of the second problem I face whenever I stand, much less take a step: pain. Standing for even a short time causes intense pain in my right foot. The pain does not go away when I sit down. Instead, it lingers and manifests into tiredness. I always know I will pay a steep price after standing for any time at all, or using my crutches too much. I might as well plan on not doing anything for the next day or so.

All of this means that when Ken told me to give my right foot some information, I knew it would send information right back in the form of pain. But I'd spent the past four days letting go, so now it was time to let go of the foot and its pain. In spite of my reservations I said, "Okay," and stood up from the weight machine bench.

"Stand up straight," Ken said.

I did not realize I stood with a natural hunch that comes from wheeling oneself around for twenty-five years. "Oops. Sorry about that," I said. I went back to what Rob had told me—to imagine that an invisible string was pulling me up through my head. I straightened up the best I could.

"Now, John, you need to tell your right leg what to do and let your legs work together. Equal and even. Don't listen to the negative thoughts telling you how you cannot do this. Just as you did on the machines, quiet your thoughts. Be totally present. Tell your legs what you want them to do."

I nodded. I took a deep breath and quieted my mind. Pain did not register as it normally did. That was a good sign, I told myself. I closed my eyes for a moment; then I told my right leg to go forward. Drawing deep inside myself for all the strength I could muster, I raised it ever so slightly and pushed it forward. The leg obeyed. I had taken a step. Before the shock of what had just happened could register, I told my left leg to move, and it did. I took a second step. Once more I told my right leg to take a step, and it did what I told it to do. Before I could tell my left leg to move I lost my balance. I grabbed hold of a nearby doorframe, and Ken helped me back to my seat.

I looked up at Ken, a little unsure of what had just happened. "Those were my first unaided steps I've taken in twenty-five years," I said. "Wow." I let out a long sigh. "That really just happened."

"It did," Ken said, smiling.

I left Ken and flew home to Sydney, then drove myself home to Penrith. "How did it go?" Amanda asked as I came in the door.

"Very good. Actually, really good," I said.

"How's your shoulder?"

I'd almost forgotten about the shoulder. "It feels better than it has in a long time. But I have something to show you," I said. I pulled out my phone and played the video of me taking my three steps.

Amanda just sort of stared at the screen, unsure of what to make of it. "Oh my God. Was this today? You took three steps. How did that happen?"

I told her the whole story.

"So what does this mean?" Amanda asked.

"Honestly, I don't really know, but I am anxious to find out."

12

Impossible

I took three steps in Ken's gym, three steps that covered about four feet total. A little over a month later I walked. My paralysis was not cured. The lesion in my spine at the twelfth thoracic vertebra that put me in a wheelchair for twenty-five years did not suddenly disappear. But I walked.

It started when Ken came down to Penrith for our next set of sessions together. He was as anxious to explore the frontiers of my walking as I was. As I've written many times, especially in the last few chapters, I believe nothing happens by coincidence. My meeting Ken is certainly no exception. Around the time I was hit by the truck, Ken started his work. He had no way to explain the phenomenon he observed in his clients until 1995. While I tackled Kona for the first time, Ken was reading a book on chaos theory by James Gleick. It turned his world upside down and gave him a framework from which to understand and explain his work. About the time I completed my third Hawaiian Ironman and started training to swim the channel, Ken started trying to get the scientific community to listen to his theories on physics and neurobiology. It took twelve years before anyone would take him seriously. Four years later I wheeled into his facility, the perfect new test subject for his ideas on how neurons work in the body. For him, my timing was perfect.

Ken also came into my life at what I believe was the perfect time. When I wheeled into Ken's facility, it was the culmination of a journey I'd started twenty-five years earlier. For two years after my accident I tried to force myself to walk, to no avail. I finally realized that paraplegia is not something you beat. That's when I had my talk with my dad when he said, "Look how far you've come just by surviving being hit by the truck. Now, how far can you go?" Answering his question pushed me to start paddling kayaks with my best mate, Johnno, which led to my first triathlon in the wheelchair, then to the Hawaiian Ironman, then the channel and the Sydney games on up to taking silver in Beijing twenty years after my accident. Chasing down one goal after another squeezed everything I could out of my body, which, Ken later told me, was part of the reason why this new chapter in my life was even possible. That's part of the equation.

Not making London and the deep disappointment that followed was just as necessary. Trying to deal with that loss led me to deep meditation, which enabled me to focus my mind and turn off the internal dialogue in my sessions with Ken. Finally, there was the phone call telling me that paddling had been added to the Paralympics. The sport I loved, the first sport I tried after my accident, was to be the sport where I fulfilled my lifetime dream of winning gold. That only seemed right. More than that, because I jumped into paddling, my shoulder started bothering me, which led me to listen to the advice of a friend who just "happened" to have experienced a new treatment.

This entire journey led me to an afternoon in a gym near my home with Ken and his assisting psychologist, Katrina. Amanda stayed home with Jack. When I left the house, I had no idea this day at the gym would be any different from what I had done every day since I returned from Emerald a month earlier. I had been following the program Ken gave me when I left Emerald, but I hadn't been pushing myself into trying to walk any more than a step or two. I expected better results again this time, since Ken was going to be right next to me, coaching me, but only in terms of tremors and pain relief. I hoped to replicate the three steps from a month earlier, and perhaps on this day I could add another step or two.

The gym where we went was one I had joined right after I returned from working with Ken in Emerald. It had similar equipment to what he used, similar but not quite the same. Since Ken knows the manufacturer of most of the weight machines he uses, he has them customize them to his exact specifications. I had to settle for what I could get in Penrith. Ken had given me a very detailed program to follow on my own, and I did my best to do just that. However, I found working his program alone in a gym filled with strangers to be very different from going through the process in his facility. I set each machine on the lightest possible setting; then I closed my eyes and manipulated the machine very, very slowly rather than pushing through a rapid series of reps. If you are not familiar with the culture inside a gym, suffice it to say this is not normal behavior. Even with my eyes closed, I could feel all the eyes staring at me. People had to wonder what on earth I was doing. The internal dialogue Ken told me to silence kicked into high gear. I sort of wondered what I was doing myself. *What are people going to think if you go into tremor?* I asked myself. *They'll think you're having a seizure and that you've lost your mind.* Soon I became intensely aware of everything around me. *Why is the music so loud? Who wears that much cologne to come to a gym? Why can't I focus?* Needless to say, my first attempts to replicate my sessions with Ken alone at the gym did not go too well.

Nor did I take any more steps on my own. I found I could

stand without pain, but I was reluctant to take more than one or two steps. I found it rather frustrating that my fear of the pain returning and not being able to balance were slowing me down. The frustration was only heightened by the internal dialogue I needed to quiet. Instead of being present with a clear mind, my mind screamed, *Why can't you do this?* while another part of me yelled back, *Easy does it or the pain will come back!* The dueling dialogues in my head only made it that much more difficult to do what I wanted to do.

Having Ken next to me in Penrith, coaching me as I sat down on the leg-curl machine, helped shut off the internal dialogue. He set the weight to its lightest setting and said, "All right, John. You know what to do. Eyes closed. Focus on being present. As you press down with your legs have each leg do its part, equal and even."

I did as I was coached. The other people in the gym who had so distracted me before just disappeared from my consciousness. The tremor came rather quickly. It soon spread throughout my body— a "global" tremor is what Ken calls them.

After a couple of hours moving about from machine to machine, Ken said to me, "Let's have you stand up now."

I got excited. The last time Ken had me stand at the end of a session I took my first three steps. "Okay," I said.

"Now, John, I want you to close your eyes and shut off the visual cortex completely. I need you to turn off all the streams of thoughts running through your head and just be present with me, right here, standing."

"I can do that," I said. I closed my eyes and tried to focus completely on the sensation of standing, just standing. I steadied my breathing.

"That's good," Ken said. "You want to be even, not too high

with excitement or too low." He paused for a few moments as I gathered myself. "John, I want you to walk straight ahead. I am right beside you and Katrina is on the other side. With your eyes closed, just start to put one foot in front of the other."

I took a deep breath. I don't know if you've ever tried walking about with your eyes closed, but it raises the anxiety level for anyone, especially someone who has only taken a few unaided steps in twenty-five years. Fear tried to take over my thinking, but I pushed it back. I focused solely on lifting my right leg and moving it forward. Doing so required my full concentration. I have absolutely zero muscle control of my right leg below the knee and very little from the hip to the knee. On top of that, I lack abduction at my hips, especially on my right side. The leg just sort of flips out and about whenever I try to move it, and I had never been able to do anything about it. But now, standing with my eyes closed in the middle of my local gym, Top 40 music blaring from above, random people moving about, the sound of weights banging in the background, I told my leg to move and it obeyed. I stepped forward with a longer stride than I had taken in Emerald a month before.

One step led to the next. And the next. Eyes still closed. Concentrating only on taking the next step, I could hear the noise around me but I ignored it. I wobbled a bit, not quite a stumble, but I regained control by moving my arms out like a tightrope walker. With each step I took, the next came that much easier. None were easy. I can honestly say that taking these steps was the hardest thing I had ever done up to that point in my life.

Ken spoke very little as I took one step after another. He just quietly let me know I was doing all right and that the path was clear in front of me. I kept stepping, walking, placing one foot in front of the other, eyes closed, my thoughts quiet. Finally Ken said, "Go ahead and stop and open your eyes."

I opened my eyes and turned toward Ken. I could not believe what I saw. I had walked at least thirty feet. Thirty! As you can imagine, I broke out in a smile. If I could dance, I probably would have then. But before I could get too caught up in the moment, Ken said, "Now, with your eyes open, walk back to where you started."

My earlier fear was replaced with excitement, but I pushed it back as well. *Not too high and not too low. Stay even*, I told myself. Thirty steps later I was back where I started. Was it easier walking back? That's difficult to say. It was obviously easier to see where I was going with my eyes open. However, without those steps with my eyes closed, I never could have walked back. I had to first shut out everything that told me I could not walk before I could truly believe that I could.

Ken and Katrina walked along beside me as I made my way back to the weight machine where I had started. A friend, Paul, who did some professional filming, followed behind, recording the moment with his camera. I did not stumble or wobble as though I might lose my balance. Instead I just walked, a little lopsided and slower than most people, but I wasn't too concerned about speed.

When I reached the machine where I had started, I turned and looked at Ken, who was beaming. If I could have jumped for joy, I would have. I reached over and grabbed Ken's shoulder. The camera records the smile on my face. It wasn't a big grin. Internally I was a bit overwhelmed and choked up, but I didn't want to break down right there, right then. I needed to process this quietly, privately. It was a lot to absorb. I held it all in, and I looked at Ken with a face that said, "I did it. Now, what's next? How far can we go with this?"

How far did not include my suddenly walking everywhere I went. After my walk from one end of the gym to the other, I got back into my wheelchair and wheeled out to my car. Mine was not, nor is it now, a Hollywood story where I suddenly get up from my wheelchair and walk and run as though I had never been hit by a truck. Perhaps that day will come. However, getting back in my chair did not diminish what had just happened. I walked thirty feet, then turned around and walked back. Paraplegics do not walk, even incomplete ones. But I just had.

Later that night I joined Ken at a birthday party for a close friend of his he wanted to introduce me to. As we got ready to leave I said to Amanda, "I'm not taking my crutches."

"What? Really?" she replied. "How are you going to put your chair in the car? What if the bathroom isn't accessible?"

"I have my walking poles. I'll be fine."

"Of course you will be!" Amanda said. "What are you going to do next? Dance?"

We smiled at each other. I looked forward to exploring the answer to her question.

When we arrived at the party, I wheeled into the house, but I spent most of my night standing and talking with people. Being able to look people in the eye rather than looking up at them from my chair was refreshingly pain-free. Standing and socializing for a couple of hours was almost as big an accomplishment as my walk earlier in the day. Those who have never lived in a wheelchair cannot understand how it feels for people to literally look down at you as you interact with them.

The next morning I woke up feeling strong. Ken, Katrina, and I headed to the gym straightaway. One of Ken's favorite sayings is "Explore and exploit." Today he planned on taking that to a new level. He put me on a leg-press machine, which he had done before. However, on this day, he had me do the presses one leg at a time, both right and left.

A good friend joined us in the gym that day. Dr. John Yeo, my spinal surgeon, came along to see what was happening to me. I asked him to be there. I called him not long after I returned from my first sessions with Ken. Dr. Yeo has been a good friend and mentor to me in the years since my accident. He was one of the doctors who patched me up and got me on my way. He also gave me my first meaningful job after my accident with Spine-Safe. Without him, there never would have been an Ironman finish or a channel swim or any of the other things I accomplished over the previous twenty-five years. That's why I wanted him there with me on this day. I wanted him to share the moment, but I also hoped he might be able to help me understand what was taking place.

I lay back on the leg-press bench and positioned my left leg in the center of the foot plate, which is more like a small sled. Even the lowest setting on a leg press is three or four times the weight of the lowest settings on other machines. I closed my eyes, turned off the internal dialogue, and pressed. The sled moved up. I pushed it to the top, then slowly lowered it down, then repeated the process a half dozen or so times.

"Now the right, John," Ken said.

I assisted my right leg up and situated it next to my extended left leg in the middle of the push plate. I held my two legs there together, just for a moment. I then moved my left leg away. My right leg supported the weight. I then slowly bent my knee and lowered the sled toward me. I controlled the descent, which was remarkable in its own right. I then told my leg to straighten, and it did. I pushed the weight back up and then repeated the process through a few reps.

"That's impossible," Dr. Yeo said with a tone that conveyed both great amazement and joy. He and Ken then fell into a discussion of how this was and was not possible. I didn't pay much attention to the conversation. All I knew is I had crossed another threshold and done that which I should not have been able to do.

After we returned to the house, I felt confident enough on my feet to do something else I had wanted to do for a long time. I walked across the living room and picked up my three-year-old son. Jack didn't quite know what to think because I had never picked him up from a standing position before. I always hoisted him up on my lap in my chair. As I lifted him up, he squirmed a bit and had a bit of a frightened look in his eye. I was sure this would soon pass. "Don't worry, Jack," I reassured him. "Daddy's got you." He kept squirming, which made me think he wasn't quite as sure that I had him as I was.

"Hey, buddy, want to have some fun?" I asked. Before Jack could answer I did something dads have been doing since time began. Dads do this. Moms do not, for reasons that soon became clear to me. I gripped on to Jack's legs at the ankles and tipped him upside down. If Jack wasn't sure what to think about my holding him, he had no doubts now. He screamed, terrified. It wasn't quite the father-son moment I had hoped for, but we got over it rather quickly. He soon grew used to me picking him up, and now he even enjoys the occasional tip upside down.

Later that evening Ken had me go out into my home gym and try out a couple of pieces of equipment Amanda had used after Jack was born: a stationary bike and a treadmill. Not long after my accident someone had given me a bike to try, one where the pedals go up and down like pistons rather than around and around on a crank. It did not work for me. Up until Ken got me on Amanda's stationary bike, that had been my last time to sit atop anything approaching a conventional bike. "Let's just see what you can do," Ken said.

What I could do was push the pedals through a cycle or two. However, because I lack abductor muscles on my right side, my right leg goes inward, and no amount of concentration can stop it. As I pushed the pedals around a time or two, my right ankle banged into the bike frame. It was not an enjoyable experience. However, in spite of my pain, this showed me that I might be able to get back on a bike someday. I just had to figure out some way to keep my foot in line, and my knee from falling in.

Then we moved to the treadmill. "Don't worry about trying to do it all on your own. It's okay if you want to hold on to the sides to keep your balance," Ken said. I took his advice and held on. "Let's see how long you can go," Ken said.

"I feel like I can go a long while," I replied.

I started walking. Again, my pace was very slow, but that didn't matter at this point. Ultimately I wanted not only to walk again but to run as well. *I'll get there eventually*, I told myself. I kept walking along, the belt slowly moving beneath me. Out of the corner of my eye I noticed Amanda walk into the garage with a friend. I turned my head so I could get a better look at her and smiled. She smiled back at me, slightly bewildered. I heard her say to her friend, nearly in shock, "John is on a treadmill, right? This is real? Wow. This is huge."

It was the first time Amanda had, with her own eyes, seen me walking more than a couple of tentative steps. I'd showed her the video of both my first steps in Emerald and my walk across the gym in Penrith, but there is something about actually witnessing an event yourself that makes all the difference. If seeing me on the treadmill surprised her, an even bigger surprise awaited both of us when we traveled to see Ken four weeks later.

13

My Gold-Medal Moment

Unless I am bum-shuffling up out of the English Channel onto the coast of France, or being carried across the sand to the water for an Ironman swim, I do not go to the beach. I never really spent a lot of time on the beach before my accident even though Sydney has some of the most beautiful beaches in the world.

I also do not go barefoot. Ever. I put on my shoes even before I get completely out of bed. I guess it's a protective instinct. Not being able to feel heat or if something sharp cut them, I've always felt shoes protected my feet.

Therefore, I had to completely abandon my comfort zone when Ken announced we were going to spend the day at the beach on the third day of our third set of sessions together. Amanda and I flew up to his place the day before. I expected to spend much of our time in the gym, just as we had both in my first visit to Emerald and when Ken came to my home in Penrith. I should have known better. The more time I spent with Ken, the more I realized that he does not like to fall into predictable patterns. The body tends to adjust rather quickly to patterns. Therefore Ken looks for ways to shock the system to continue to produce different results. "Explore and exploit" means truly exploring, discovering new ways to uncover the potential inside.

On this day, explore and exploit meant going to Broadbeach on the Gold Coast, a little over five hundred miles north of Sydney in the state of Queensland. Ken had moved to the Gold Coast from Emerald in the two months since I first came to see him. Broadbeach is just south of Surfers Paradise, which gives you an idea of what the beaches are like. Arriving there brought me face-to-face with one of the difficulties of life for a wheelie: sand and wheelchairs do not go together. Two months earlier this problem might well have been insurmountable. Not today.

I wheeled as far as I could down a paved walking path. When we reached the end, Ken said, "Take off your shoes and socks, John. We're going out there."

"To the water?"

"Yes."

"You're the boss, mate," I said with a grin. I took off my shoes and socks. Amanda and I gave each other a knowing sideways glance and a lift of the eyebrows as I stood up on the warm sand. Amanda handed me my walking poles. Using the poles to keep my balance, I walked about three hundred feet through the thick sand. I stumbled a few times but Katrina or Ken caught me, holding me up until I regained my balance. Once we reached the harder, wet sand left behind by the receding tide, I laid aside the poles and walked on my own to the water's edge. "Step into the water until it laps up over your feet," Ken said. I waded in until the water came up just above my ankles.

"Now, here's our plan for today, John. I want you to just stand here. Close your eyes, feel the breeze on your face, listen to the sound of the waves, and let go. I want you to really engage with everything you experience with your visual cortex turned off. Try to put your mind in sync with nature. Feel it. Experience it. Shut out everything else."

I steadied my mind, closed my eyes, and tried to just be. The sun shone down on my head; the wind blew cool across my face. Waves moved up and down on my legs as they bounced up onto the shore. Gulls called out to one another above me. People laughed in the distance as they played and splashed in the water. I didn't try to analyze anything. Instead I let myself experience it and become one with it.

The point of Ken's exercise was less about getting me in tune with nature and more about building on the progress we'd made over the past few months. As each wave washed onto shore, it pulled the sand beneath my feet out to sea. To stay upright I had to make very small, almost imperceptible adjustments with each foot. These tiny movements were strengthening the neural connection between my brain and my feet and legs. The fact that my toes responded to the moving sand at all was completely new for me, and not a response I was consciously controlling. For years I had hoped to see any movement in my right foot, the slightest twitch in my toes—anything to let me know my foot wasn't just drooping down at the end of my leg. As the sand rushed about on my foot, my toes instinctively gripped down on the sand, even on my right foot. Like I said, the movement was so slight that one had to look close to see it. Ken saw it. And so did Amanda.

Amanda was standing off just to one side of me. She didn't say a word to me or do anything to disrupt my concentration. No one spoke but Ken, and only then did he speak very infrequently. Time slipped by, but I didn't notice. I went into a deep meditative state. Later Amanda told me Ken had said I might be there a while, so she went for a walk down the beach. She was surprised when she returned sometime later and found me standing in the exact same place without moving.

After I stood in the water for an hour, Ken had another surprise for me. "You said you wanted to walk and *run*. Well, today we're going to run!" he said. "Are you ready?"

"Absolutely," I said. "But once you get me going I may not stop, you know."

Ken laughed. "That's what I like to hear," he said. We moved up from the water a bit to a place where the sand was a little dryer but still flat enough not to trip me. Ken drew a line in the sand with his foot. "There are no expectations here. Every single step you take is a step in the right direction no matter what happens. You may just take off because there is a history that says you can do that. We're just going to get moving toward that space. So, if you are prepared for it, step up to the line and let's have a go of it."

I took a step toward the start line Ken had drawn in the sand.

"Close your eyes for a few seconds. Get the thought in your mind"—that is, about what I was about to do. "Get ready. See yourself running, and just enjoy the ride, mate. Once you step over that line, it's on," Ken said.

"I'm actually looking to run," I said with a bit of a laugh. I had dreamed of this moment for so long, and now it was about to happen.

"Okay," Ken said, as though we went out on the beach for a run every day.

My mind flashed back to the hours upon hours of meditation I had done six months or so earlier. In them I felt the ground moving quickly beneath my feet and the wind whipping through my hair. In my mind I had already taken off in a sprint. That's the place where I put my mind as I stood on the line in the sand. I did not wonder if I could run. I knew I could. Now I simply had to have my body do what my mind had already seen. I let out a deep breath and shook my arms out. I could not stop grinning.

"I've seen your legs doing it in the gym," Ken said. "You've got to back yourself."

I let out another deep breath. *Here goes nothing*, I thought to myself and took off. After I took my first step Ken said, "Go."

I took off running, arms pumping, legs churning as quickly as I could move them. Ten steps later I fell on my face. No one rushed over to help me up. Ken said, "That's a good fall."

I looked up at Amanda. Her eyes looked like a lost mother who could not help her child that had taken a fall. But she didn't say a word. She didn't cry out or rush over saying, "Oh my God, John, are you okay?" Later she told me she was afraid my right foot might catch and my weight falling over it would break it. But she kept those thoughts to herself. Instead she let me work through this on my own in my own way.

I pushed myself back up onto my feet and said, "Well, that wasn't quite the result I was looking for. Let's do it again." I walked back to the line.

"Bring your arms lower to your body this time," Ken said.

When I was ready, Ken shouted "Go," dropped his arm, and I took off again. Ken, Amanda, and Katrina kept pace with me. Ken continually said, "Go, go, go." Twenty-five steps later I lost my balance and tumbled onto my left side. I had a big grin on my face. I could feel it. I knew this was really going to happen. Ken laughed a triumphant, "Yes, you are doing this!" kind of laugh.

I bounced up off the sand. "Once more," I said.

"All right, get back to the start line. This time keep your knees up high," Ken said.

I couldn't wait to try again.

Ken asked, "Are you ready, John?"

"Yes," I said.

"All right, go!" I took off. I passed the point where I fell the first time. Then I sprinted past the place where I fell the second time. Arms pumping. Knees high. Ken kept pace, telling me over and over, "Knees up. Head up. That's the way. Nice. Go." Amanda and Katrina started cheering me on. I sprinted down the beach with everything I had in me. "He's only a local lad, but look at him go!" Ken yelled, after seventy yards or so. That broke my concentration and made me smile, just before I hit the sand for the final time.

I looked up. "I ran. I actually ran," I said to Amanda as she came over, helped me up, and gave me a hug.

"You did! It was awesome!" she said.

"I was running on the beach, baby. I was *running on the beach*!"

"I know, I know!" Amanda said, laughing.

Turning to Ken, I asked, "So what do I do now?"

"You once told me you wanted to go for a walk on the beach with your wife. Here's the beach. There's your wife. What are you waiting for?"

I looked over at Amanda. I had dreamed many things, but I never really dreamed this moment was possible. To walk hand in hand with my wife down one of the most beautiful beaches in the world—the very thought took my breath away. I reached over and took hold of her hand. As I did I felt those sparks you feel when you first hold the hand of someone you love. The moment was magic.

We took two, maybe three steps when Amanda said, "Hang on, John. Don't hold my hand like that. Here"—she moved my hand over hers the way she wanted it—"like this."

I stopped. "Really? Are you serious?" I started laughing. "First time I'm walking on the beach with you and you're going, 'You're holding my hand the wrong way'? Does it really matter?"

"It wasn't right the other way," Amanda said.

We laughed. "Well, let's make sure we get it right for the first time that I walk on the beach in twenty-five years!" I said.

Amanda shot back with a smile, "There's no point in doing it wrong. I don't want you forming bad habits, you know!"

"Well, all right, then." I gripped her hand the way she wanted, and we both had a good laugh. But Amanda was right about my not knowing how to hold her hand. This was the first time we had held hands with me in an upright, walking position. I had always reached up from my chair. The position of my hand is very different reaching up than it is reaching across. Our silly, wonderful conversation showed we both knew we had moved to a place where we could experience life together hand in hand and face-to-face, not always with me in a chair looking up, but standing and walking beside my wife.

I can honestly say that the walk along the beach with my wife was my gold-medal moment. Nothing I had ever accomplished in sports, or ever hoped to accomplish, could compare. We walked along, hand in hand, and all I could think was, *This is what I have been searching for my entire life. Anything I could ever do in sports, anything I could ever do for* me, *does not compare to this moment of sharing my life with my wife and family.* Maurie was right all those years before. Life is not about me. It means so much more when it is about us.

After our day on the beach, I wanted to see the video footage of my run. Ken waited two days to pull it out. I could tell he and Amanda were a bit nervous about my seeing it. "What's the problem?" I asked. "I really want to see it."

"Just keep in mind that what you did out there was amazing. Very amazing," Amanda said.

I thought her comment a bit odd until I saw the footage. In my mind, I was running. I pictured it a bit like the opening scene from *Chariots of Fire*. I felt I had good form, arms in, knees high—a beautiful sprint. Then I watched the video. My "running" didn't look anything like I imagined. It didn't really look like a run at all, at least not for anyone else. I shook my head. "I really thought I was running," I said.

"Compared to your walk, you were sweet," Amanda said.

"I don't know," I said.

"There's no comparison between this and your walks in the gym," she said. "Does it compare to the way you once ran on the football field? No. But don't let that take away from what you did out there."

In spite of Amanda's encouraging remarks, I was a bit down the next day. It took a while to realize she was right. Compared to my walk in the gym, I was running. But I wanted to run as I once did. When I was a young man, there were none faster than me on the football field. My legs were my greatest strength. I always believed I was never out of any race as long as I had my legs under me. That's where I wanted to be now. The video showed me how far I still had to go. I wondered if I would ever get there.

However, I did not allow myself to dwell on these thoughts for long. To do so would be so counterproductive that I might not make any further progress. I could not dwell on what I had lost in my accident. Instead, to go forward, I had to focus on what was available to me now and make the most of it. Come to think of it, that's pretty much been my philosophy for everything in my life. I think it is a pretty good way to live, and it has served me well.

I spent a week with Ken, while Amanda had to leave after four days to get back to Jack. Before she left I made sure Amanda got to go to the gym and experience the tremor therapy for herself. My reasons were twofold. First, I wanted her to fully understand what was happening to me, and the only way to do that was to experience it herself. Second, and ultimately more importantly, she had some back pain that had bothered her for a while, along with an intermittent pain in her chest that had puzzled all her doctors. She caught on to Ken's methods quite quickly. In no time she went into a full global tremor. The process worked almost too well on her. Back at home on our way out of the gym she went into aftershocks. The tremor so took over that she had to lie down on a mat until it passed. Afterward her back loosened up and her chest stopped hurting, although the chest pain came back a few days later.

After Amanda returned to Penrith, Ken surprised me with a new shock to my system, something I had not done since I was a child. "I want you to climb up on the trampoline," he told me.

Ken didn't expect me to climb on, stand up, and start jumping about, not on the first day, at least. He started me off with push-ups. Most of you have probably done conventional push-ups, as have I, but attempting them on the constantly moving surface of a trampoline was something else entirely. I struggled to do a dozen that first time on the trampoline. However, by the afternoon I was doing sets of twenty at a time.

After the push-ups, Ken had me get up on my knees, then up to my feet. Getting onto my feet was hard enough. Remaining upright was nearly impossible. Just as he had done on the beach, Ken had me stand with my eyes closed. Over and over I lost my balance and tumbled onto my side. Each time I got back up. "Relax, John. Get comfortable up there. Let go of whatever is going on internally." Eventually I got to the point where I could stand. Of course, that was only the beginning. By the end of my time in the Gold Coast with Ken, he had me bouncing up on the trampoline, falling back on my bum, and bouncing back up onto my feet. I felt like a little kid. This wasn't therapy. This was fun!

I bought a trampoline when I got home. It sits in our backyard today, and Jack and I spend time playing and bouncing together. I never thought anything could compare to walking down the beach with my wife, but this is a very close second. For twenty-five years I never thought I would get out of my wheelchair. Now I am bouncing on a trampoline with my son. It's like winning the gold medal every day.

14

Two Steps Back in Paradise

A few weeks after my stroll along the beach with Amanda, Ken came back to Penrith for one last session before Amanda, Jack, and I left for a dream three-month stay in a beach house in Lanikai, Hawaii. I wanted to spend as much time with Ken as I could before the trip so that I might squeeze as much out of myself as possible. Three months is a long time to go between sessions, but given the progress we'd made thus far, I felt confident I could continue building on my own. Ken likes to keep things shaken up to keep my system from growing too accustomed to any one set of exercises, and this trip was definitely no exception. "We're going to the mall," he announced.

Walking on a beach is one thing. Walking inside my local shopping mall in front of many curious eyes is another. However, by this time I had grown confident enough in my walking that I was ready for more people to have a look. "I'm game," I told Ken. "What do you have in mind?"

What he had in mind was the escalators. I hadn't stepped on a set of escalators since before my accident. I also was a bit hesitant because on escalators, the ground moves underneath you. Once you are on the stair portion, all you have to do is stand. However, at the top and bottom are the flat pieces where you must step on quickly with both feet. In spite of my reservations, I told Ken I was up for anything. I even made a phone call before we left to give myself a little extra motivation to make it up the escalators.

Our friend Paul had been present with his camera at most of my sessions with Ken to document the process. When we arrived at the mall with Paul in tow, we were stopped by security. "No filming allowed," we were told. I explained what we had in mind and why the camera was there, but my explanation fell on deaf ears. Paul had to turn off the camera. Ken and I walked across the mall to the escalators in the center. My gait is a little different from most people's. I guess you could describe it as a bit of a limp. If anyone noticed as we walked through the mall, they didn't care enough to stop and stare. We walked along just like any other two shoppers.

At the base of the escalators, Ken gave me a bit of a pep talk. "Stand up straight, step forward, and have a ride of it," he said. "There's really nothing to it."

I looked down at the flat moving belt at the base of the escalators. It looked like something to me. I looked up at the top and knew there was only one way up there to the appointment I had made. "Here goes," I said. I stepped out with my right foot and then quickly brought my left beside it. I looked about as the stairs carried me up, and enjoyed the view. I felt like a little boy riding up for the first time.

As I neared the end of my ride I turned toward the front and focused all my attention on my dismount. The top stair flattened out. The conveyor belt moved me forward. I raised my right foot and then dropped it down on the solid ground in front of me. My left foot followed. I took another quick couple of steps from the momentum I had from the escalators themselves. Ken looked up at me from below. "Nice ride, mate. I knew you could do it."

I gave him a wave and a smile, then turned and walked toward the coffee shop just up the way. Up ahead I saw that my appointment was already there, waiting for me, although he hadn't yet seen me. I stepped through the door of the coffee shop. Johnno looked up. "Hello, mate," I said with a broad grin. The look on his face is one I will always remember. Tears filled his eyes. He jumped up and came over to me. I looked him in the eye, face-to-face, having walked up to meet him for the first time in twenty-five years. "It's something, isn't it?" I said.

Johnno grabbed me and gave me a hug. We both had tears in our eyes now.

Every day I grew more comfortable with life on my feet, so much so that when it came time to leave for Hawaii, Amanda and I decided to leave my crutches behind, instead opting to take the walking poles. Although I gave up trying to walk any distance on the crutches back in 1990, I still used them for getting in and out of the car and on airplanes to move about. However, since I started working with Ken, I had, for all intents and purposes, laid my crutches aside completely. I saw no reason to drag them to Hawaii with us, not even as an emergency backup in case I had a setback. I've never been one to worry about setbacks. The cursed Canadian crutches remained in Australia while Amanda, Jack, and I flew off for our three-month stay in Lanikai. I planned on getting rid of them once and for all after we came home.

Leaving the crutches behind felt like crossing over another barrier, as though I had left a piece of the damage of the accident behind. I could not wait to get to Hawaii and see how much farther I could go during our three-month holiday in paradise. I didn't have to wait until we arrived to find out. A couple of hours into the flight I decided to stretch my legs and go to the bathroom. A bit later I came back to Amanda and Jack. I was beaming like I'd just qualified for Rio. "I've just been to the bathroom for the first time on a plane not using crutches," I announced. This may seem like something small to you, but it was a huge moment for me. I finally felt free. I think I sort of floated above my seat the rest of the flight I was so happy. With such a great moment of victory on the flight, I could not wait to see what the next three months held in store for us.

The first couple of days in Hawaii were exactly as I had hoped they would be. On the third day, Amanda and I went out in our backyard to throw a football around while Jack was off to his first day of preschool on the island. Ken had actually recommended this exercise to us as a way of developing my balance. He also wanted me to do this barefoot to toughen up my feet and engage sensory stimulation. I didn't much care for the barefoot part, but the man had gotten me up and walking. I wasn't going to argue with his methods now.

The grass in the yard was sea grass and more coarse than ours back home in Penrith. The scene, however, was amazing. Our grass ran down to a strip of sand. Beyond the sand lay the Pacific Ocean. I could think of no better place to toss around a football.

Rather than throw the football straight to me every time, Amanda threw it just to my right or my left. The idea was that this forced me to move laterally, something I had trouble doing. "Have a go at this," she'd say as she heaved it to me. For a girl, she has a pretty good arm. I had to dive for a few, but not many. We laughed and talked and had a great time throwing the ball around the yard. I never imagined I'd get to do such a thing. The only hard part was the grass and my bare feet. After all the years of disuse, the bottoms of my feet were soft like a baby's, completely free of calluses. They were ill prepared for a day of moving about on coarse grass.

I paid the price the next day.

I woke up and immediately could sense discomfort in my right foot. The sensation was very different from what I had experienced for so many years. I lifted my leg up to have a look to see if I could figure out what was going on. There, on the bottom of my big toe, was an enormous blister. I am not exaggerating when I say it was the size of an American half dollar. Another set of smaller blisters covered part of my heel. "Amanda, come have a look at this," I said.

She took one look and said, "Oh, that's not good."

I did not realize at the time how big a setback these blisters truly were. I could not put weight on my right foot, not because of my spinal cord injury, but because the blister agitated my hypersensitivity and sent pain messages shooting up my leg. Living on the beach didn't help. We tried protecting the blister with a large-size bandage, but that didn't work. Sand crept in under the bandage when I went swimming. I tried a silicone sock over just the toe. I had the same problem. Looking back, I suppose the toe may have healed faster if I had been content to sit in the house in front of the television with my foot propped up. But we were in Hawaii, in a house right on the beach. There was no way I was going to waste my time on a couch waiting for a blister to go away.

The blister on my toe kept me from walking, so I went back to using the wheelchair inside the house. Amanda went to the local pharmacy and purchased a set of traditional crutches for me to use to get myself in and out of the water and over the sand. I did not let my inability to stretch the limits of my walking get me down. We had two spare bedrooms in our house, and we had friends and family coming in and out for the whole three months.

When I wasn't entertaining friends, I was on the water. A good friend Randy lent me two outriggers, a two man and a single. I trained every day in the single. I struck up a friendship with a local who happened to know the under-18 paddling world champion. He agreed to help me with my technique. Other paddlers were all around me. Lanikai is basically a paddler's paradise. I spent hours on the water, but the time flew by. Time wasn't the only thing flying. My brother-in-law had measured and marked up a two-hundred-meter course in the inlet for me. We spent hours doing time trials. During one training run on the course, I matched the world record time for my event. With more than two years of training still to go, I felt like I was on the right track to seriously consider Rio.

I didn't confine my paddling to the course, though. Just off of Lanikai Beach, and right out my back door, are two small islands known as the Mokes. Waves come up between the islands and the shore and create great surf. I paddled out in the middle of them and caught some waves. Basically, I was surfing in an outrigger canoe.

One afternoon the wind changed while I was out paddling, and the waves that came rolling in were the best yet. I rode wave after wave, staying out on the water much later than usual. I looked around at the waves and thought about calling it a day. Instead I said those three little words that always get you into trouble: "Just one more." I watched the waves coming toward me. A big one was coming my way, so I turned and paddled hard to get on top of it. As soon as I got high up on it, I knew I was in trouble. The wave kept building and building until it suddenly threw me down in front of it and crashed down on top of me. It pushed me under the water. Unfortunately, I had attached the Velcro ankle strap fixed to the outrigger. The boat was now filled with water and going down fast, taking me with it. *Oh, this is not good*, I said to myself. All of my meditation training kicked in. Instead of panicking I stayed as calm as one could possibly stay while going under the water, strapped to an outrigger canoe. Finally, the force of the water stopped pulling the boat under, and I managed to reach down and rip the Velcro ankle strap off. At last I was free from the outrigger, but I was still far under the water. I swam toward the light above me with all I had. At last my head bobbed above the water. I filled my lungs with oxygen. No breath of air ever tasted so good.

Once I was on top of the water, I was able to survey my situation. My outrigger was coming to the surface as well, albeit in four pieces. I swam over and retrieved my paddle, since it was also borrowed. I stuffed it down the back of my pants. I looked around. The closest Moke island looked to be about three-quarters of a mile away, not that it would do me much good beyond getting out of the water. The Mokes are nothing but rock with a small strip of sand surrounding them. I could see my house off in the other direction. Getting there meant a two-and-a-half-mile swim. *Okay, so what am I going to do now?* I said to myself. I knew the answer. I had to go for a swim. I couldn't stay where I was.

I was about to swim toward home when I spotted a guy in a fishing boat off the rocks on the island farthest from me. He had a runabout pulled up on the sand. I started waving my paddle, and fortunately he saw me. He started pulling his line in and signaled that he would head my way. He came over in the small aluminum runabout. After he pulled me out of the water I asked, "Can you help me gather the pieces to my boat? It doesn't belong to me. I borrowed it from a friend."

"Sure," the fisherman said. On the ride toward my house he told me how he'd been stranded out in the same area once. "As soon as I saw you I knew I had to help," he said. I thanked him, but I also wondered if he hadn't been helped if he would have just let me swim the two and a half miles on my own.

Eventually we reached the shore by my house. I'd left my wheelchair sitting on the edge of the grass just above the beach. "Whose wheelchair is that?" he asked.

"Mine," I replied.

"No way, man! You're out surfing the waves in the Mokes and you're in a wheelchair? That's crazy, dude!"

I guess he was probably right. It was a little crazy, but it sure was fun. My mother-in-law, Karen, was visiting and came down to the beach as the fisherman was dragging the pieces of my outrigger onto the sand. She had been checking her watch, knowing I was overdue to be back. She was relieved that I had managed to get a lift back but was more than a little bit shocked at seeing the boat in four pieces.

Once we returned home from Hawaii, my foot finally started to heal properly. I started working on walking again, but I also continued focusing heavily upon paddling. I raced the Australian champion a second time. He'd beaten me by a second before I left for Hawaii. In the rematch I beat him by three full seconds. My goal was clear.

15

"Which Do You Want More?"

For twenty-five years my wheelchair was an inseparable part of who I was. While I refused to accept the label *disabled*, if someone asked who I was and what I did, I'd reply, "I am John Maclean, Paralympian," or "John Maclean, wheelchair athlete." I realize for some, those labels are synonymous with what is termed disabled, but they never were for me. Disabled means less than, and I proved throughout my sporting life that I was in no way less than anyone. And I've come to realize the same holds true even if I had never competed in any sport. No wheelie is less than anyone else, nor is any person who lives with what some call disabilities. Every person alive faces daily challenges we must overcome to succeed. Some are simply more visible than others. My chair was my physical reminder to everyone of the challenges I faced, but rather than hide it I learned to embrace it.

In the two years immediately following my accident, I never thought I could possibly grow so comfortable with my chair. I hated it in the beginning. I hated the way people looked at me in it. I hated being shorter than everyone else. I hated having to rely on other people to do things for me that I couldn't do for myself. But once I came to peace with the fact that I was never going to get my old life back, I quickly discovered my chair set me free to race into my new life. Eventually it simply became a part of me, so much so that if a fire alarm goes off in the middle of the night, my natural reaction is to bounce into my chair and wheel out the door (after grabbing my wife and son first, of course).

Reaching this level of acceptance was a good and healthy thing for me. No one can ever go forward if they cling to the past. I had long since released my football-playing, I-can-outrun-everyone-on-the-field self. Once I did I went farther, faster, than I ever dreamed possible. I saw no reason this had to stop. I still had a gold medal to win, with new challenges and new possibilities waiting for me beyond that.

I was quite secure in who I was and how I saw myself until I wheeled into Ken's gym a short time after returning from Hawaii. Our three months in Lanikai had been everything we had imagined it might be, but real life was waiting for us when we returned. Our house in Penrith had sold. Amanda and I didn't have much time to find a new place to live somewhere in the Sydney area, however. Amanda's father had battled health issues for some time, and he took a turn for the worse not long after we returned to Australia. Amanda wanted to spend time with her father in New Zealand, and when he passed away in early December she remained to be with family while I looked after Jack, before heading over for the funeral and Christmas.

During one of her brief stays back in Australia I made a quick trip to see Ken. The wounds on my feet had finally healed, and I was anxious once again to move ahead with my walking. I wheeled in, and Ken and I started talking about my time in Hawaii. "It was wonderful," I told him. "I fell into a group of paddlers over there who helped me immensely with my techniques." I went on to tell him the biggest development of all: that I had matched the world record time in my event during a training run on our makeshift course. "I could not have done this without you, Ken. My shoulder feels better than it has in years. I think I am only scratching the surface on what I can achieve."

Now, before I tell you Ken's response, please remember that I originally went to him because of my shoulder pain that hindered my paddling. If I had never climbed into an outrigger with the goal of bringing home a gold medal from Rio, I never would have gone to see him once, much less multiple visits of four and five days at a time. While walking had been my goal since my time at the health retreat following the disappointment of missing out on the London games, I had no idea Ken could help me get back on my feet when I first went to see him. I went to him for pain relief, nothing more. Walking was an unexpected, happy discovery.

After I told him about my progress with paddling, Ken asked me, "What do you want more, John? Do you want a gold medal or do you want to walk?"

The answer was obvious. I wanted to walk more than anything else. However, up until this point, I never saw this as an either/or proposition. "Obviously, walk," I replied. "But why do I have to make a choice?"

"It all goes back to your internal dialogue and what you believe about yourself, how you see yourself."

"Okay," I said, a little unsure of where he was going with this. As I wrote earlier, I am quite comfortable with who I am.

"Here's the question I want you to think about, John. Who are you, really?"

I thought about his question for a moment. "Go on," I said without answering.

"You came to me to help you achieve your goal of a gold medal. The pain in your shoulder threatened your goal, but now the shoulder is better and now you are able to push yourself and go faster than you could before. You just spent three months paddling in Hawaii. Now your sights are set on winning gold in the 2016 Paralympics, and that goal seems very achievable."

"Yes. This is all true."

Ken leaned over and looked me in the eye. "But is that who you are, John? Are you John Maclean, Paralympian? Because, you see, when you define yourself in those terms, you are still defining yourself by who you were six months ago, before you took your first three steps in my gym, before you ran on the beach, and before you walked hand in hand with your lovely wife. Are you still that same person today?"

"Because if that is how I see myself, that is who I will continue to be," I said.

"Well said," Ken replied. "Now, if winning a gold medal is what you want most out of life, very good. You are on your way. But I think we've only just begun to explore and exploit the parameters of what you can do on your legs. Your wheelchair is the default position for you. It's easy to go back to default. Very easy. But if you want to reset your default, you must first change what you believe about yourself. That's the choice you have to make. Which do you want more, to walk or to win a gold medal?"

In a way, this conversation reminded me of the conversation I had with my father on the day I embraced my wheelchair, the day I realized paraplegia is not something you beat. "Look how far you've come," my dad said. "Now, how far can you go?" I had gone further in my chair than even I ever imagined possible. Ironman Hall of Fame. First athlete to swim the English Channel and complete the Hawaiian Ironman. Olympian. Two-time Paralympian. Paralympic silver medalist. In essence Ken was now telling me the same thing. *Look how far you've come already in your chair. Now, how far can you go on your legs?*

But did this have to be an either/or equation? Why couldn't I see how far I could go on my legs while also pursuing my dream of winning a gold medal? I wrestled with this question for a while, even after I thought I had answered it. Again, the choice was easy. I wanted to walk and I wanted to run. But I also loved paddling. The camaraderie with my fellow paddlers at home on the Nepean River and in Hawaii with so many friends was not something I wanted to give up. My times with Johnno in our kayak so many years ago were some of the best memories of my life. Gold was certainly my goal, but the sport was more than that for me. I loved it. I enjoyed rowing to a degree, but paddling was completely different. Giving it up was a far more difficult decision than what I imagined during my conversation with Ken.

I returned home to Penrith. We had to be out of the house in a few weeks, which meant we had to find a new house. Because we had so little time, we decided to look at rental properties rather than find a house to buy. One rainy afternoon Amanda and I set out to look at a couple of places our real estate agent had found for us. Jack stayed with a sitter. We didn't want to drag him out in such foul weather. I didn't look forward to it myself. If we hadn't had our backs against the wall in terms of when we had to be out of our house, I might have tried to push the appointment back a day or two. But since we didn't have the luxury of time, Amanda and I made the hour-long drive into Sydney in the rain.

We drove up to the first house the realtor had for us to see. The rain grew heavier and heavier. I parked on the street outside the house. Amanda turned to me and said, "See you in there!" She jumped out of the car and raced up to the porch and into the house as quickly as she could to keep from getting soaked, leaving me with the umbrella to make my way at a slightly slower pace. Eventually she came back to the front door to check on me. I was out of the car, but I hadn't gone up to the house. Instead she found me standing on the driveway. I looked over at her with a huge grin on my face. Amanda shouted over the rain, "Come on! What are you doing?"

Then it hit her: I was walking in the rain holding an umbrella, something I could never do in a chair. She smiled and laughed when I made it to the house.

"How good is this!" I said, giving her a hug.

We went inside the house for the home tour. All the while I kept thinking to myself, *This is the difference between going for gold and walking.* The choice isn't about grand achievements and medals but about my daily quality of life. *Which do I want more, a gold medal or to walk?* The choice was starting to get easier.

Since Ken's first visit to Penrith, I had continued toying with Amanda's stationary bike. I had managed to get one revolution with the pedals, which led to another and another. However, I could not go for long because my right ankle banged into the bike frame. Since I couldn't keep my foot from turning in on my own, I decided to look for other solutions.

I talked to an engineer friend, John Roach, and asked if he could adapt a pedal that would keep my ankle free of the bike. He built a wedge that my entire foot could rest on. We experimented with several models until we found one that worked reasonably well. I liked it so much I had him do one for the left side as well. Although I could control my left leg a little better than I could my right, concentrating on keeping my left foot in line used up energy I preferred to use pushing the pedals up and down.

With the new pedals in place, I found I could get a good rhythm going on the stationary bike in our garage. One day while riding the bike I started to wonder, *What would happen if I put these pedals on a regular bicycle?* I decided to find out. We were a little over a week from moving away from Penrith when one evening Paul, a close neighbor, and I transferred the pedals to Amanda's bicycle. I, obviously, did not have a standard bike of my own. Paul and I managed to attach the pedals, but I did not immediately jump on and go for a ride. I wanted Amanda to be there. The next morning I said, "I'm going to go for a ride on your bike."

"My real bike?" she said, still in bed.

"Yeah. Paul helped me put the pedals John made for me on it. I'm going to try to take it for a spin."

"Well, just wait; I need to get Jack sorted. I want to see you ride it, and I'll get the video camera," Amanda said.

"Sure, sure," I said. "I will wait for you." I put on a pair of cycling pants to protect my bony bum and went outside to wait for Amanda.

But of course, I didn't wait long. I tried, I really did, but standing in the garage, staring at those pedals hanging off of that bicycle, I was a little boy on Christmas morning. That little boy finally could wait no longer. I pushed the bike out into the street in front of the house. I couldn't just throw my foot over and go. Instead, I had to push the bike over next to the curb. I stood on top of the curb and placed my right leg over the bike and situated my foot on the pedal. I then attached a strap over the top of my foot to hold it in place. With my right foot strapped in, I started pushing myself along the curb with my left, trying to build momentum. One of two things was going to happen. Either I would ride off down the street, or I would fall over. If I fell, I planned on jumping back up and trying again until I got the result I wanted.

I gave myself one last big push and set my left foot up onto the pedal and pushed down hard. The handlebars wobbled a bit as I moved away from the curb into the street. I started cranking the pedals, building up a little speed. I broke out in a huge smile.

This really was Christmas morning. "How good is this?" I said to myself. "I'm riding a bike!"

I pedaled to the end of our street, ecstatic. Although I had logged thousands of miles, literally, on my handcycle, riding a conventional bike is a completely different experience. A handcycle sits low to the ground, the pedals right at eye level. On the newer models, the rider has to nearly lie down. Now I was sitting up high, pedaling away. My arms hardly knew what to do with my legs now doing all the work.

I was having so much fun pedaling down the street that I forgot that the hardest part of my first ride was just ahead. My street dead-ends. When I reached the end, I would have to turn around. Suddenly I flashed back to the first time I rode a bike as a little boy. Turning is much more difficult than just going straight. I slowed down a bit and tentatively turned the handlebars. I felt very wobbly on the turn but managed to stay upright.

As I started back up my street, Paul had just gotten off his bike and was changing his shoes to go for a run when he saw me ride by. "John! You're doing it! Oh my God! You're riding a bike!"

That nearly did me in. My concentration broke for just a moment, and I nearly fell off. *Focus, focus!* I told myself. *Don't fall.* I regained my balance and managed to stay upright.

"I didn't realize you were going to try and ride this morning!" he said.

"Well, you know," I said, grinning like the Cheshire cat. The two of us had a chat as he ran alongside me. It was as though this were something the two of us did every day, as if we had just done it the day before.

I reached my house, pulled over to the curb, and climbed off. I went inside. "The pedals worked," I told Amanda.

"What?" she said.

"They worked. I rode your bike up the street and back."

"I thought you were going to wait for me."

"Well…" I stammered. "I couldn't."

Amanda was not surprised. "I guess that's to be expected," she said. "Was it okay?"

I just smiled. I couldn't find the words to describe what I felt inside. Honestly, I truly was a little boy who just received his first bike. The fourteen-year-old me, the one who rode his new bike until he was too exhausted to even put it away at night, came out. As I rode up and down my street, a switch flipped inside of me. All at once it was as though I had never sat down in an outrigger or kayak and never touched a paddle. The sport suddenly no longer existed for me. I'd returned to a much older love, and I could not wait to explore and exploit, to see how far I could go.

I rode back up and down the street several times that day. As I rode along, a question came to me, one I knew I had to pursue with everything in me. *I wonder*, I asked myself, *if it is now possible for me to go back and do a triathlon, not in a wheelchair but as a conventional athlete.* The thought should have struck me as crazy. Instead it felt like the next chapter of my life was about to unfold.

16

From Peter Parker to Spider-Man

Very soon after riding a conventional bike for the first time, I called an old friend, Gordon Bell. Gordie and I go back to my first attempt at the Hawaiian Ironman in 1995, when he made sure I was included in the Australian contingent. I didn't know any of the guys, but Gordie pulled me into the club. He even had an Aussie flag strapped to my racing chair. Right before the race began, in the water, Gordon was close by when a guy yelled out, "Hey, you can't wear a wet suit!" Before I could say a word, Gordie answered, "He's in a wheelchair, you idiot." Two years later, in the 1997 Ironman, Gordon and I crossed the finish line together. It wasn't anything we planned. The two of us just happened to finish at the same time. Gordon was now the race director for the Nepean Triathlon, which is why I called him.

"I wanted to let you know I would like to enter the triathlon this year," I said.

"That's great, John. You know how much we love to have you in the race. Any time you can make it, we want you here," Gordon replied. I've done the Nepean several times beyond those mentioned previously in this book.

"Thank you," I said, "but I'm not asking as a wheelchair athlete. Gordie, this year, I would like to enter as a conventional athlete."

"What?" Gordon said, very, very confused.

"I said I want to enter as a conventional athlete."

"Okay. Wait. What? I mean, uh, John—how?"

I gave Gordon the condensed version of what had happened over the last several months. Up until this phone call, I hadn't made a secret of regaining substantial use of my legs, but I also had not gone out of my way to let people outside my circle of family and friends know about it.

"Wow," Gordon said, obviously stunned. "That's extraordinary, John. Please keep me up to date as to what you want to do."

"Right now, my intention is to do the triathlon in October, eight months from now. So if you could allow me to race, then we'll put it all together and see how it goes," I said.

"Of course, John," Gordon said. "You can race however you want to race."

I hung up the phone and knew I had stepped over a line into a new normal. First, I had now, in my own mind, moved from "John Maclean, wheelchair athlete and Paralympian" to "John Maclean, aspiring triathlete." And my first triathlon had to be the Nepean, the very race for which I was training at the time of my accident in 1988 and the first triathlon in which I competed as a wheelie six years later. The 1994 Nepean proved to be the springboard for everything that followed. Now, here I was twenty years later, ready to go back for another new beginning. The same questions I asked myself in 1994 I asked myself now: If I can do the Nepean, then what else is possible? How far can I go with this?

I had also already started thinking about ways to do more with the triathlon than simply compete. If I could ride a bike thirty kilometers, or eighteen miles, after a one-kilometer swim, then get off the bike and walk ten kilometers, or six miles, then this would truly be something newsworthy. I began to envision the upcoming Nepean Triathlon as the perfect fund-raiser for my foundation, while also opening a whole new discussion about what is possible for those with physical challenges. Walking was no longer just about me. I started the John Maclean Foundation because I wanted to make a difference in the lives of children in wheelchairs. On my feet, competing in a triathlon as a conventional athlete, I now had the opportunity to make the greatest impact yet.

After I got off the phone with Gordon, I made another couple of calls. I needed to find good homes for a couple of pieces of equipment I no longer had any use for. I called one friend and offered him my racing chair. I gave the handcycle to another. I've always believed if I was going to do something, I was going to give it 100 percent. As long as the racing chair and handcycle sat in my garage, I had an out, a way to default back to the comfortable and familiar. In order for me to give my all as a conventional athlete, I had to burn my bridges, so to speak. Now I was committed. There was no turning back.

As if "burning my bridges" didn't solidify my resolve to complete the Nepean Triathlon as a conventional athlete, I took it a step further when I mentioned my plans during an interview with a reporter from Australia's *60 Minutes*. They were doing a feature for the show on my learning to walk again. I just sort of blurted out the triathlon when she asked me what was next for John Maclean. It is a very common question. Every time I speak, people always ask me what I am going to do next. My friends even do it. Before I decided to enter the Nepean, friends had already started talking about me going back to Kona to do the Ironman.

Since everyone else asks what I am going to do next, it only made sense for *60 Minutes* to do the same. During the actual broadcast, they did not include me talking about the Nepean

Triathlon, but at the close of the report the host added, "We wish John the best of luck as he trains for the Nepean Triathlon in October of this year." With that, there was no changing my mind or backing out. My course was set. It was Nepean or bust.

The *60 Minutes* piece was a turning point for me in other ways as well. My walking had not just gone public; it was now a national news item. The *60 Minutes* report began with me in my wheelchair, rolling along a pier on Sydney Harbour. It ended with me "running" one hundred meters while the reporter clicked off my time with a stopwatch. In between, viewers met Amanda and Jack along with Ken Ware and my spinal specialist, Dr. John Yeo. Clips included my sporting past, all of which built up to the video of my first three steps with Ken. The reporter took Ken and me back to the beach to recreate my first run, as well as put me back on a trampoline to show what I could do there. It ended with Amanda and me together. The reporter said, "I get the feeling you are incredibly content with where you are."

"Life's fantastic," I replied. "I have a beautiful wife and an amazing little boy. What more could you ask for?"

"And you are up on your feet walking," she said.

"Yep. I am a walking man," I said.

Almost immediately our phones blew up with e-mails and text messages. I had to ignore mine because I was in Las Vegas for a speaking engagement. I hadn't even seen the report when the calls started, since I had to wait several hours to be able to view the show online. By the time I saw it, Amanda had already been besieged by calls and texts and more e-mails. Many people contacted us just to congratulate me. Others e-mailed to inquire about my treatment, and more still requested to have me come and speak to their group. Several people wanted to know more about the John Maclean Foundation and how they could get involved.

If the *60 Minutes* piece sealed my decision to do the Nepean Triathlon, it also confirmed my idea of using it to benefit the foundation. I began to think this could be our greatest fund-raiser since I launched the foundation.

Now that I had fully committed myself, I had to face another question: Could I actually do this? I knew I could swim one kilometer without a problem. As I wrote earlier, once you swim the English Channel, you figure you can pretty much do anything in the water. I also felt confident I could handle the eighteen-mile bike ride. In addition to riding Amanda's bike, I spent a good bit of time on the spin bike. Soon I wouldn't have to steal my wife's bicycle. Dave Richardson from Panther Cycles, a bike shop in my hometown of Penrith, who had looked after me and my handcycles for years, had generously offered to custom-build a new bike for me. With the right equipment, I knew I could do anything, especially with six months to train before the race.

The problem was what it had always been. Twelve months earlier I took three steps then lost my balance and had to stop. Six months ahead I planned on walking six miles after pushing my legs to propel a bicycle eighteen miles. From three steps to six miles in eighteen months, I didn't know if it was possible. I wondered if I was a little crazy to try. My doctors also expressed some concern. Because of my lack of abduction at my hips, they tend to twist out of alignment, and my right leg is shorter than my left. Taking short walks did not seem to pose any danger. However, there were questions about short- and long-term damage I might do to myself after walking six miles. Amanda and I used to joke with one another about it. We'd say, "Well, what's the worst that could happen? I guess I could end up in a wheelchair for the rest of my life." Since I had already lived out that scenario, I figured I had nothing to lose.

A solution presented itself immediately after *60 Minutes* aired my story. As I wrote earlier, for as long as I can remember, people have come into my life at just the moment I needed them most. When a particular e-mail arrived, I knew it had happened again. A man named Darren Pereira wrote to us via my website. "I've just watched *60 Minutes*," he said, "and I found your story to be very inspiring. I work for a company called Neuromuscular Orthotics. We are a world leader in the prescription, design and fitting of a type of orthosis called a 'Stance Control Knee Ankle Foot Orthosis.' The SCKAFO has worked particularly well with spinal cord injuries and neurological clients to improve their walking. We have over 100 clients with this type of orthosis and I believe John would benefit greatly from it. If he'd like to call me up, I'd love to get together with him and see what we could do."

Amanda was the first to see Darren's message. She forwarded it to me in Vegas. When I returned home, I immediately called him and set up a meeting. In the meantime, we did a little research into his company and their work. From the start, this appeared to be another of those coincidences that always seem to arise for me at just the right time. Darren's company was located in Melbourne, Australia, which is a little over five hundred miles south of Sydney. It took a few weeks to coordinate our schedules, but I was finally able to go spend time with him and get fitted for the latest in carbon-fiber leg braces.

The difference in ability between my legs dictated different types of braces for each. Even though I always try to be "equal and even," as Ken preached to me, the fact of the matter is my legs are not equal. After a series of tests, Darren fitted my left leg with a dynamic ground-reaction ankle-foot orthosis, which fits under my foot and runs up to just below my knee. The brace uses two carbon Kevlar rods, which stabilize my ankle while also giving me some spring in my step to assist my weak calf muscle group.

On my right leg, Darren used a SCKAFO that used a stance-control orthotic knee joint from Horton's Orthotics & Prosthetics, a company in Little Rock, Arkansas. The brace runs from under my foot to above my knee. When I put weight on my heel, the Horton knee joint locks to prevent my knee from collapsing. Then, as I move forward, the joint unlocks and lets me swing my knee freely for the next step. The lower section also immobilizes my foot and ankle, the foot and ankle that want to flop down. This gives me more stability as I walk.

Darren needed three weeks to manufacture the braces for my legs, which was followed by many adjustment sessions to fine-tune everything and get it just right. The results were, for me, mind-blowing. The only way I can describe the difference the braces made to me is this: Without them I am Peter Parker. With them I am Spider-Man. Taking even one step requires such great effort, both physically and mentally, that if someone came up and started a conversation with me while I was walking, I might fall over. The braces give me much greater stability. My knees and feet are aligned and supported, which lets me just go. When I combined the leg braces with my walking poles, the type hikers use when traversing up and down trails, I believed I had found the key to beating the walk leg of the triathlon. Like I said, before my braces I was Peter Parker. With them I am Spider-Man.

Around the same time I received my braces, I got a phone call from Dave at the bike shop in Penrith telling me my new bike was ready. I cannot describe my excitement. This was my third new bike in my life. My experience with the first two hadn't gone so well. The first, you may recall, was stolen from in front of my house after I'd had it all of one day. The second was under me when the truck hit me on the M4. Two strikes against me just meant my third bike was going to be the one where I would see my greatest success. After all, my third attempts have often proven to be the charm. It was that way when I competed in the 1,500-meter racewalk as a boy, and with Kona.

When I got to the bike shop, it was love at first sight. The bike was customized and the black frame had the words John Maclean Foundation emblazoned across it. The shop had also fitted the bike with the pedals my friend John had designed for me. "Let's have a go at it," I said. I drove the bike to the road used in the bike leg of the Nepean Triathlon. For the most part the road is flat. However, there is a hill on the edge of town that I knew was going to be my biggest challenge. I thought I might as well tackle it right from the start. I dropped my new bike into a low gear and pedaled with all I had. When I reached the top of the hill, I immediately turned around and coasted back down it with a grin from ear to ear. Even though I had never pedaled anywhere close to eighteen miles, I knew right then I was going to be able to do the bike leg without a problem.

Once I had my bike I began experimenting with wearing my leg braces while riding it to keep my ankles clear of the frame. Even with my customized pedals, my legs, especially my right, had a tendency to clip the frame from time to time. Darren made a few adjustments, and the braces became a part of my riding gear.

With my new bike in hand, I called Johnno. "I'm going to come out and ride with your cycling group," I told him. He and a few of his mates got together on Saturdays and rode around the roads close to where I used to live. Most of them were training for some-thing, an upcoming triathlon or Ironman, but more than anything they went out to have some fun then stop for a coffee along the

way. The first time I joined them I knew I had made the right decision in ditching my paddle for a bike and pushing toward doing
the Nepean Triathlon. Back when I used a handcycle, Johnno and I
logged many, many miles together. He and I went out on the M4 a
few years after my accident as we trained for my first Nepean Triathlon in my wheelchair. When I trained for the Ironman, Johnno
often joined me as a training partner. But in all those rides over so
many years, the two of us had never looked over at one another
and talked on the same level. When I rode my old handcycle, he
had to look down at me and I always had to call up to him. On my
new bike we were on the same level for the very first time. It was a
wonderful experience.

As I explored my newfound freedom on my bike, I ran into
one problem. Amanda and I had moved to the town of Haberfield,
which is part of the greater Sydney metropolitan area. Just over a
half mile from our home is Iron Cove, part of Sydney Harbour. A
popular walking and riding path called the Bay Run crosses over
the Iron Cove Bridge to form a five-mile-long loop. One afternoon
I decided to tackle the Bay Run for a training ride. Most of the
trail is flat. However, the trail becomes quite steep on the climb up
to the bridge.

Since I had conquered one hill already, I thought I should be
able to manage the two on the Bay Run. Once I got out on the
trail, I realized I forgot to factor in the other cyclists and runners.
The Bay Run is very popular with us fitness-minded Aussies. I
took off riding and was having quite a good time, when I came
upon a group of women walking and talking. They were spread
out across the path and weren't paying much attention to anyone
else. As I came up on them a thought flashed through my mind:
Oh no! You can't stop this thing without falling over! Because of
the way I have to strap my feet into the pedals, I can't just stop for

a moment, put a foot down on the ground, and wait for the traffic to pass. Once I am moving on my bike, you cannot tell there's anything wrong with my legs at all. But the only way I can stop and start is to lean against something for balance.

Thankfully, I managed to navigate around the first group of talkers I came upon, and the next, and the next. When I reached the rise leading up to the bridge on Victoria Road, I started to get very nervous. Falling over here wasn't really an option. On top of that, once I got up on the bridge, I had to deal with the car traffic on the other side of the pedestrian path while also avoiding other walkers and bikers coming at me.

When I got home, Amanda asked, "How was your ride? You weren't gone as long as I thought you would be."

"I don't think I am quite ready for the Bay Run yet," I said. For a while, at least, I spent most of my time riding back in Penrith, forty-five minutes away, especially on the flat trail around the Penrith Lakes, where the Nepean Triathlon was going to be held. Every time I climbed on my bike, though, I felt that much more confident leading into the triathlon. I could not wait for the challenge to arrive.

17

Too Big to Fail

The first indication of the magnitude of what was to come with my triathlon attempt came while I was in Las Vegas just over five months before the actual race. In my speaking engagements with business audiences, I usually stick to a similar story line. My presentations take the audience along my varied achievements in sports, often built around my father's words, "Look how far you've come. Now, how far can you go?" At the end I always challenge the audience to set big goals for themselves and then map out strategies for reaching them.

However, I added a new twist to my Vegas presentation for an IT company. At the end of my presentation in front of 1,500 people, I unveiled my latest achievement by standing up out of my wheelchair and walking across the stage. That brought the house down. Now that I had their full attention, I added, "In October I'm going to attempt the hardest thing I've ever done in my life. I'm going back to where my journey began and attempting the Nepean Triathlon as a conventional athlete. I don't know if I can do it, but I'm going to give it all I've got." Then, almost as an aside, I added, "You're welcome to come to Sydney to join me. We're going to get as many people as we can to come out, not just to support me, but to help raise money for children in wheelchairs through the John Maclean Foundation."

In response, a company-wide sales incentive was announced. The winners would receive a five-day trip to Australia culminating in the Nepean Triathlon. They could compete or they could just come out in support. The incentive turned out to be a big hit, and in the end over thirty employees came over from the States for the event.

After the success in Las Vegas, which is only 7,700 miles from Sydney, I decided to make walking across the stage and inviting people to come join me at the Nepean Triathlon a regular part of my presentations. People responded, especially in Australia. Along with asking people to come join me, I and my foundation staff called companies with whom I had relationships and asked them to come on board as event sponsors. Many responded. Dimension Data, a longtime supporter of the John Maclean Foundation and of me personally, not only wrote the foundation a sizable check, but they also had a large team of employees sign up to compete in the triathlon. Hyundai signed up to sponsor the triathlon effort and made a long-term commitment to the foundation. Even my old football club, the Penrith Panthers, stepped up and joined the effort.

As more and more corporate sponsors came on board, more people signed up to join me in the triathlon. Gordon Bell set up a special category for people registering to race for the John Maclean Foundation. A triathlon starts participants in groups, called "waves," based on their age and ability, from professionals on down. The organizers set up an additional wave for this event, the JMF wave. They promoted the foundation in their materials leading up to the race. Because not everyone is physically able to do a triathlon, we created another way for people to get involved.

People could sign up just to walk with me on the second of two laps (just over three miles) around the primary lake at the regatta center at Penrith Lakes. In additional to the 150 people who were doing the whole triathlon for JMF, another three hundred people signed up for the walk. What started as an idea that came to me as I pedaled around my old neighborhood on my wife's bicycle was growing into a movement.

Through my career, I have competed on some very large stages. Just twenty-eight miles down the road from the site of the Nepean Triathlon, I raced wheelchairs in front of 115,000 people at the Olympic Games in 2000. That race didn't turn out so well, as I recall. However, even though the crowd was huge, the number of people in the stands who were there just for me was fairly small. A large group of my family and friends flew to Beijing for the 2008 Paralympic Games, but altogether they numbered around fifty. But nothing I had ever done elicited the kind of response the foundation and I did with my upcoming triathlon. On top of all the people who came out just to support the foundation and cheer me on, friends from around the world called to tell me they were going to fly over and join me in the race. David Knight, who now lived in New York, promised to be there, as did a friend of mine, Tim, from Boston and another from Vancouver. Johnno wouldn't miss it, although his commute wasn't nearly as far. Amanda's brother Calvin and my brother Marc and his family from New Zealand were committed. Even my brother Don and his wife, Kelly, planned to fly over from Toronto. Don had been with me in Kona as well as the channel swim and Beijing. He told me there was no way he was missing *this*, which, in terms of the wow factor, outdid them all.

After hanging up the phone with another friend who committed to come to Australia to support me, it hit me. This little triathlon of mine had grown too large for me to fail. I could not let all these people down. However, unlike everything else I had ever attempted, I honestly did not know if I could actually pull this off. Twenty years earlier when I attempted to become the first wheelie to do the Nepean Triathlon, I knew I could do it. My training rides with Johnno in the months leading up to it far surpassed the distances I faced in the triathlon itself. The same was true of Kona. While the severity of the winds and the difficulty of the course surprised me my first time over, I felt very confident going in that I would indeed finish. And I did. Three times. Even when I dove into the English Channel, I knew I could swim thirty-plus miles in open ocean. I had done more than that in a single attempt during the 1,100 miles I swam in the eight months before the actual channel attempt.

But this was going to be different. I tried "training" for the walk leg, but it proved difficult. Amanda and I walked two and a half miles one day in the park across from our Haberfield home. I felt great while Amanda and I walked. She was like, "You know what? Look what you can do without even really training." Our high spirits took a hit when we got home. When I took off my shoes, I discovered large blisters, especially on my right foot. I was also very tired from the effort. Two and a half miles, a measly four kilometers, was less than half of what I would have to do on the day of the race. I told myself that after training I would do better, but the sores on my feet made me wonder how much real training I could realistically do. If I tore up my feet before the actual race, I might have to drop out. That was not an option. My dilemma was then how to train without doing damage. I went back to Darren for some adjustments. Beyond that there wasn't much I could do.

I forgot all about training after Amanda came home from a doctor's appointment. For some time she'd had on-again, off-again chest pains. Over the past year the pains had grown in frequency and intensity. She went through a series of tests at the end of 2013 after we returned from Hawaii, but they all sort of took a backseat when her father took a turn for the worse. When she finally made it back to her cardiologist, she assumed he was going to refer her on to another specialist. Never in our wildest dreams did we expect the diagnosis Amanda received. She had a coronary artery anomaly in her heart, which she had been born with. The anomaly caused blood flow to sporadically slow, which resulted in angina-type pain. Our first question was, what now? The doctor could not tell us.

What followed was more than six months of opinions from a variety of cardiologists and heart surgeons, all with varying views. Apparently her condition was quite rare, and doctors don't often come across it—at least in living patients. The condition is known to result in sudden death; therefore, it was usually discovered in otherwise healthy people who had died suddenly. Some doctors told us we should do nothing. They didn't want to do open-heart surgery on an otherwise perfectly healthy forty-four-year-old woman as a preventative measure for something that might never happen. On the other hand, we had doctors warn us that she might get up one morning and simply fall over dead. Amanda is a very no-nonsense kind of girl, and such indecisiveness drives her crazy. The uncertainty also thrust our entire family into limbo. Amanda had finished working just before we went to Hawaii. I was now the primary provider for the family through my speaking engagements. She wanted to look for a new job, yet she could not until we knew whether or not she was going to have to have surgery. On top of that, every time she had a pain, it threw her into a bit of a panic. Headlines like "Toddler Found Playing Cars on Top of Dead Mother" flashed in her head. She always kept her phone with her.

Finally, Amanda decided to have the anomaly bypassed

through open-heart surgery. Then came the challenge of finding the right time to do it. Since the *60 Minutes* story aired, my speaking schedule had taken off. I had engagements in both Australia and overseas that we had to dance around. We finally just picked a date, but then Amanda came down with a bronchial infection. We delayed the surgery while she went through a round of antibiotics. Then we had to delay it again. And a third time.

When she finally was able to get in and have the bypass, they scheduled the operation for the exact same time as a speaking engagement I had in Sydney for a group of over five hundred. I immediately planned on canceling, but Amanda wouldn't hear of it. "You're not going to cancel. They booked you months ago. This is too short a notice," she insisted. When I tried to argue, she told me, "I'll be here when you finish. Go. Do your thing. Then come up to the hospital."

Her spirit just showed why I love her as I do. She didn't plan on anything going wrong in the operation. Amanda had absolute confidence that she would come out of the operation well and would just need time and care for recovery. She had no fear about something going wrong on the operating table. She just felt that, as far as open-heart surgery goes, this was a routine operation, and she had one of the leading heart surgeons in Australia. As it turns out, she was right. I spent time with her the night before, and as I was preparing to leave for the city to go and do my presentation, she was in preop. By the time I finished, she was out of surgery, in intensive care, and doing fine. She made a full and speedy recovery.

As we got closer to the race, I had two consistent training partners join me as I prepared: Steve Waugh and Jock Campbell. My good friend Steve Waugh may be unfamiliar to my American audience, but in Australia, he is the Michael Jordan of cricket, a former Australian captain. And cricket is huge over here. Jock is a former Australian cricket team trainer. He has especially made his mark as a strength and fitness coach.

Steve, Jock, and I got together as training partners thanks to Toyota. They had a film crew follow us around in the weeks leading up to the race and through the triathlon itself. They turned our sessions into three short films. Because Steve was on the same level I was as a swimmer before my first Nepean in 1986 (the year I basically dog-paddled a full kilometer), we spent more time in the pool than we did anywhere else. At one point I just had Steve grab hold of my legs and I dragged him through the pool. We joked that he was going to do this during the triathlon itself. We also went on several bike rides and short walks.

To appreciate the enormity of this development, I need to take you back to my first Nepean Triathlon in my wheelchair. Johnno and I rode mile after mile after mile to build up my strength not only to complete, but to compete. I didn't want to just finish. I wanted to show I was the equal of any other athlete out there. This same drive followed me to Kona and the channel and everywhere else I went. Now, for the first time in my life, I understood that just finishing was going to be a huge victory in and of itself. Yet finishing remained the big if for me. I truly was going into this race trying to answer the question, is it possible?

Three weeks before the race, I drove out to Penrith and met Johnno at the regatta center, site of the Nepean Triathlon, for a practice run. I needed to see how close I was to being able to do what I had boldly proclaimed I intended to do. We didn't keep our test run a complete surprise. Several of his training mates who were friends of mine as well came out.

I wanted the test run to be as close to the real thing as possible.

We set our bikes up in the parking lot that was to become the staging area for over 1,500 bicycles on race day. I also got one of my friends who runs the Penrith Lakes facility to set up a chair for me on the ramp leading up out of the water where the swim leg would end. The walk from the swim leg to the bike staging area covers the length of two or three football fields. I can walk that far without my braces, but I prefer not to. I put my braces and walking poles next to the chair.

Johnno and I and the rest of the guys jumped into the water a little ways back from the end of the swim portion. I didn't see much point in swimming a full kilometer. After all, the swim was not going to be the problem. Thinking back to my first Nepean in 1986, I had to laugh. Back then I could hardly swim at all, but I knew however far behind I fell, I could make it up on the run. Now the swim was the only portion where I felt fully comfortable.

We swam a couple of hundred yards to the ramp. Back when I competed in triathlons as a wheelie, Johnno and someone else carried me up out of the water. This time around, when we reached the water's edge, he gave me a look like, *Am I supposed to pick you up or what?* "I've got it," I said. I started to stand up and walk up the wet incline, but I decided against it. Instead, I crawled up on my hands and knees. A couple of the guys looked like they wanted to come over and give me a hand. I waved them off. "Believe me, guys—this is the easiest way for me," I said to them.

I crawled up the ramp and after putting on my braces and shoes, I grabbed my walking poles and said, "Let's go for a ride."

"Sounds good, mate," Johnno said. "Lead the way."

The bike leg of the Nepean leaves the regatta center, heads up the road running alongside it, then turns north at a roundabout on the main road leading out of Penrith. On race day all traffic is blocked, giving the athletes full use of the road without having to look over their shoulders for cars. Since we didn't have that luxury, Johnno and I did two laps around the main lake, which comes to six miles. Three weeks later I would have to do these same two laps on foot. The flat ride on the bike was more relaxing than a training exercise. We talked and laughed as we sped around the lake. The fun ended when we got off our bikes.

We parked our bikes back in the staging area. "You sure you want to do this, Johnny?" Johnno asked.

"Yes. I need to do at least one lap," I said.

"All right. I'm right here with you," he said.

I took off my bike helmet and grabbed my walking poles for the walk back down from the staging area to the walking path that goes around the lake. The trail starts off with a climb up the rise of the bridge that goes over the part of the lake that connects the section where races are held and the old lakes that have always been there. Together the lakes form a loop, with the old lakes serving as the warm-up area. The bridge itself is rather impressive, with the Olympic rings right in the middle.

After one or two steps up the bridge, I felt discomfort. It increased with the next step and the next. I knew I was in trouble, and we had barely begun. Even without looking at my feet, I knew blisters were growing on both of them. I didn't stop to take off my shoes to take a look, but I knew they were there.

Johnno and I walked along. He chatted a bit, but I didn't answer. I stared straight ahead, concentrating. *Right pole, left leg. Left pole, right leg*, I told myself over and over. The happy guy on the bike who was out for a bit of fun with his friends on a Saturday afternoon was long gone. The pain kept building. I pushed it aside as best I could and kept moving forward. About halfway around our one lap Johnno finally said, "You're not saying anything, Johnny. Are you all right?"

"I'm fine," I lied. I didn't say much else until we reached the end of the trail and started back toward our cars.

As we were coming around at the end of the one lap, a guy rode by on a bike. He stopped and approached me. "Are you John Maclean?" he asked. He was wearing a John Maclean Foundation bike jersey from one of our earlier fund-raisers.

"Yes," I said.

"I thought it might be you," he said with a smile. "I just wanted to let you know that I have followed your career, and you have inspired me. Thank you."

"No, thank you," I said.

"Do you mind if I snap a photo of us together?" he asked.

"Sure," I replied.

The two of us chatted for a few more minutes as he snapped a few selfies with me. My new friend's timing was perfect. By the time I reached the end of that practice lap, I was spent. I was experiencing transferred pain from my feet and my back ached. An internal dialogue bounced through my head, asking how I was possibly going to be able to do the full triathlon when just half the distance had worn me out. Yet, as I came to the finish line, here was a man who reminded me of why I was going to attempt to do that which should have been impossible. This wasn't about me. By getting out of my chair and completing this triathlon as a conventional athlete, I hoped to push the boundaries of what was possible. I hoped to inspire others to take their eyes off their limitations and go beyond all they ever imagined was possible. More than anything, I wanted to touch the lives of children in wheelchairs, those who were growing up hearing all they could never do. I wanted them to look at me and say, "If John can do that, nothing will hold me back either."

My new friend's encouragement gave me the lift I needed. However, the question I hoped to answer with my practice run still hung over me. Was it possible for a man who spent twenty-six years in a wheelchair to get up and do a triathlon as a conventional athlete? I would find out soon enough. If the answer was up to me, then it was going to be an overwhelming "Yes!"

18

Race Day

I woke up a little after three on the morning of the triathlon. I hoped finally to find the time to go to a quiet place within myself to mentally prepare for the race. Up until this moment, quiet eluded me. The weeks leading up to the Nepean had been some of the most hectic of my life. Normally, when I go into a huge competition, I follow a very regimented training schedule. I peak in my physical workouts a few weeks before the actual event. Then I move my focus to the mental preparation I must have to compete at my best.

The lead-up to the Nepean was anything but normal. I had not been able to train at the level I felt I needed to prepare myself for the single greatest challenge of my life. With so little physical training, my mental preparation became that much more crucial. Unfortunately there was no time for that either.

The madness began right after Johnno and I went on our practice run. A day or two later I jumped on a plane to fly to Hawaii for the Ironman at Kona. Race organizers invited me to speak to all the Ironman contestants at a dinner before the race. They showed a clip from the *60 Minutes* piece, then had me say a few words. Afterward Bob Babbitt, cofounder of the Challenged Athletes Foundation, radio host, and Ironman Hall of Famer, did a question-and-answer session with me. The first question was simple enough: "What words of encouragement do you have for the athletes, especially the first-timers?" I talked about my own first experience and made a couple of jokes about the wind on the course. I will never forget that wind. Then I was asked, "What do you have coming up?" That gave me a chance to talk about the Nepean Triathlon and my attempt to do it as a conventional athlete. Finally, I was asked, "Do you see yourself ever coming back here to Kona?"—that is, not as a guest but as a participant. The crowd cheered over that one. I replied, "Well, I'm just learning how to walk. I've got my first conventional triathlon coming up, so I just want to take it one step at a time." This wasn't the first time I had been asked about doing Kona as a conventional athlete. Friends back home ask me about it all the time. Even Ken mentioned the possibility during our sessions together.

A full schedule awaited me upon my return from Kona. I had a few speaking engagements, then Amanda and I both got caught up in making sure everything was ready for the hundreds of John Maclean Foundation folks who were coming out for the triathlon, either to race or to do the walk. Racers were to receive jerseys, while walkers would receive JMF T-shirts. Both were emblazoned with the logos of all our corporate sponsors. While the foundation has an excellent manager who takes care of such matters, I found I still got caught up in questions about their arrival. Everyone was also to receive a hat, but those were delayed. I wasn't quite sure if they would make it in time for the race.

One week before the race, the real craziness set in. Mark, my collaborator on this book, flew in from the States the Sunday before the race. The two of us found time to do a couple of laps around the Bay Run on bikes, but I did not find time for the quiet reflection I needed to prepare mentally for the race. Mark and I started right off working on the book, laying out the chapters, talking about the structure. He wasn't going to be in Australia long, and we needed to make the most of our time. Then Monday night I had to go into Sydney to stay at a hotel where I was scheduled to make a breakfast speech the next morning for a business group. As soon as that speech was over, I rushed home, changed clothes, and then ran out to Penrith to drop my bike off at the regatta center and take one final look at the course. Then it was back home to throw a few things into a suitcase and go back into the city for a dinner with a group of primary school principals. I stayed in Sydney that night. First thing the next morning I spoke to the Primary School Principal Association at their annual conference, then went straight over to Dimension Data's offices to give a pep talk to the employees who planned to run the triathlon with me four days later. No sooner had I finished speaking than I had to get back home, change again, and head off to the beach at Cronulla. Steve Waugh and Jock Campbell met me there for another film session with the crew from Toyota.

The next day, Thursday, kicked off with my phone blowing up. The Sydney *Daily Telegraph* did a front-page feature on my quest to do a triathlon as a conventional athlete. This is the equivalent of having the *New York Times* or *USA Today* do a front-page story. In Australia it may even be bigger. As soon as the papers hit the newsstands, national sports channels started calling to set up interviews. I was still on the phone when I went out to the airport to pick up my brother Don and his wife, who had just flown in from Canada. They settled into my house just long enough for them to catch their breath. Then we all headed off to the beach community of Watsons Bay for lunch with David Knight and his mom. David had flown in from New York. After lunch it was time for a little sightseeing before heading out for an appointment with Darren, who had come into Sydney for the race. He did a couple of adjustments on my braces in the hopes of alleviating my problems with blisters. I tried to find a quiet moment while he went into his shop to grind off a little of the instep, but I fell asleep instead.

Friday was also a whirlwind. Amanda and I spent a good deal of time with Ken and his wife, Nickie. It was our first chance to reconnect with them since the *60 Minutes* piece aired. I had more interviews to do throughout the day, which were followed by more time with family. My brother Marc along with his family, as well as my sister Marion and Amanda's brother Calvin, were all in town for the big event.

By the time Saturday rolled around, I was pretty well exhausted, which was not good since the race was the next day. Amanda and I loaded up both of our vehicles with a variety of friends and family, along with our luggage and my gear, and drove out to Penrith. After checking into our hotel, I tried to catch a little alone time, but more friends who had come in just for this event were also at the same hotel. They wanted to see me, and I wanted to see them as well. I also needed to go out to the triathlon site to check on some last-minute details. I kept telling myself, *I'll still be able to catch come quiet time in a bit. I'll have time to calm my mind and prepare mentally,* but that time never came. Saturday night we had a small family reunion over dinner at the Penrith Panthers Rugby League Club, which includes a wide variety of restaurants. I broke away from the family gathering as early as I could, but more phone calls awaited me when I got back to the hotel.

Now here I was wide-awake at 3:45 on the morning of what I knew was going to be the most difficult thing I had ever done in my life. Amanda was in the next room. Jack had stayed at home with a close friend, Ashleigh, who would bring him out to the race later in the morning. I slept out in the front room of our suite, as I knew I might have trouble sleeping and would be up early. Lying back in the bed, I tried to start the process of mentally going through each leg of the race, of visualizing what I needed to do. Since I could not really train for the six-mile walk, I basically had to tell my legs we were going to do this and give them no choice but to obey. Unfortunately, I could not calm down my mind.

Grabbing my phone, I fired off a text to the only person I knew who was always up at this hour. "Get out of bed. It's going to be a great day," I wrote.

My phone buzzed almost immediately. "You need to get up earlier than that, brother, if you want to get up before me."

I laughed and hit the call button. Johnno answered on the first ring. "Hey, Muz," I said, using the nickname I had for him.

"Johnny, you're up already?" Johnno asked.

"I couldn't sleep. Too much adrenaline, I suppose."

"It's going to be a big day," he said.

"That it is," I agreed.

"A lot of people are coming out to support you," he said.

"I know," I replied.

"And Amanda and Jack are going to be with you," he said with a tone that said far more than his words.

I paused and fought back tears. Johnno and I had been through so much together, going back to our days as two young football players on the Warragamba Wombats. He was the one who came to the hospital more than anyone whose last name wasn't Maclean. Once I came home from the hospital, he was there, pushing me as we became training partners. We got lost together in the dark on the Nepean River in our kayak; then he carried me in and out of the water for my first triathlon as a wheelie. The two of us had shared so many more moments over the years—he supported me at

Ironman, stood and delivered a speech at my and Amanda's wedding, and the two of us crossed the finish line in his first Ironman just a few years earlier. He, more than anyone else, knew what it meant to me to have Amanda and Jack share this moment.

"Muz." I paused, fighting to hold it together. "None of this would have happened without you. I am so grateful for your friendship." I could not say anything else. Emotion overwhelmed me.

I could tell the moment got to my old friend as well. He just said, "I will see you soon, mate," and hung up.

After hanging up with Johnno I slowly opened the door into Amanda's room. "Are you awake?" I asked softly.

"Yes; come in," Amanda said.

I crawled up into bed next to her and wrapped my arms around her.

"How are you feeling?" she asked.

"Good," I said.

"Wow, what a huge day. It is finally here. You're going to do a triathlon," she said to me.

"Yes, I am," I said.

"Are you ready?" Amanda asked.

"I have to be," I replied. What other choice did I have?

We arrived at the regatta center before the sun was up. Although the JMF wave was to be the last to start, I had much to do before I climbed into the water for the swim leg. Wally, my close friend and support swimmer for the channel, had come in during the night and met us at the hotel before we left. He rode over with Amanda and me. He did not enter as a competitor. Instead, in classic Wally fashion, he came simply to do whatever Amanda or I needed him to do throughout the day.

People were already buzzing about when we arrived at the site of the triathlon. From the moment I got out of the car, I had to wear two hats. In one, I was John Maclean the triathlete, just another of the 1,500 who had turned out for this, Australia's oldest triathlon. Unfortunately, I could not put on that hat until I actually waded into the water. Until then I had to be John Maclean, host of all those who had come out to support the John Maclean Foundation. Ricky Jeffs, chairman of the foundation, and our CEO, Tiffany, did an incredible job pulling everything together to make the day happen, including getting the hats to the site in time for the race. But since the foundation bears my name, I am its face. And on the day so many people had come out to support me and my foundation, I had to play the role of host.

Before I kicked into full host mode, I did a final check of my bike. One of the guys from Panther Cycles was already there. "Let me take a look at it," he said. The next time I saw my bike it was waiting for me in the bicycle staging area. The bike guy adjusted the derailleurs, brakes, and every other moving part, making sure everything was in perfect working order. With my bike ready, I made my way up a hill to where more JMF competitors had started to gather.

Amanda and I went up the hill together, just the two of us, I in my chair with her walking alongside. A morning layer of clouds made it seem earlier than it was. We didn't say much. This was the closest I came to a quiet moment before the start of the race. I was thankful to have it and even more thankful that Amanda was with me. Before every race I have entered, before every great challenge, I have had an image in my head of what I wanted to accomplish. In Beijing, I pictured Kathryn and me on the top step of the podium with gold medals hanging around our necks. When I dove into the English Channel, I pictured myself lying on the sands of France, soaking up the moment of triumph. Since the day I committed to doing the Nepean as a conventional athlete, all I wanted to do was walk across the finish line holding hands with Amanda on one side and Jack on the other. I didn't care about my time. Honestly, how could I? Nor did it matter to me how many or how few other people were there. Don't get me wrong—I am very grateful for the massive support I received from so many people. But more than anything, I wanted to share this moment with my wife and little boy. If they had not been there, I wouldn't have been either.

Ricky came over to me as we reached the sign-in area. "Looks like it's going to be a big day for you and JMF, Johnny," he said. "I can't believe the response."

"Do you have the numbers for how much it looks like we will raise today?" I asked.

"It should come in around a quarter of a million dollars," he said with a huge smile.

"Wow," I said. "That's incredible." In addition to having people come out and join me for the triathlon, we also planned to present grant checks to five families in need of support for their young wheelies after I crossed the finish line. We wanted people to see exactly whom they were supporting on this day.

Ricky and I talked for a few more minutes. Then I remembered something I needed to do. If I was going to compete, I needed to sign in. I wheeled over to the registration area. "Which wave?" the triathlon volunteer asked until she looked up at me. She broke out in a big smile. "Oh, John, it's great to have you with us today," she said. Digging through a box of envelopes, she pulled one out and handed it to me. Inside I found the ankle bracelet that would electronically mark my time as well as the other assorted items I needed as a competitor. Even though I had planned for this moment for months, putting on the ankle bracelet and affixing my number to my shirt brought home what was about to happen. *I'm really going to do this!* I said to myself.

After leaving the registration area, I spent the next hour or more greeting people. Over and over I stood from my chair to shake hands and talk with people eye to eye. I probably should have sat more and conserved my energy for the race, but that was the last thing on my mind at the moment. So many people had come from all over the world—the least I could do was stand and thank them.

The PA announcer in the background called a group to the start line. The JMF wave still had a little while to wait. When it looked like most of our people were together, they all gathered near the JMF booth we'd set up where people could receive their jerseys, T-shirts, and hats. Ricky called for everyone's attention. He said a few words about the day; then it was my turn to talk. As I looked out at all of them, incredible gratitude came over me. "I want to thank all of you for coming out and supporting me and the kids our foundation reaches. This is a day I've looked forward to for a very long time. I guess you could say this is a day that's been twenty-six years in the making. I plan on going out and finishing something I started a long time ago. Thank you for being here to do this with me."

With that, my host duties were officially over until the end of the race. After more handshakes and greetings, everyone made their way down a hill and over toward the starting area on the long lake where the rowing competition was held fourteen years earlier during the Sydney Olympics. Eventually most everyone had left me except Amanda and Wally. I heard the PA announcer call another group to the start line. We were next. "I guess this is it. I need to get down there," I said.

"Yep, off you go," Amanda said, and gave me a kiss. "See you in transition."

I let out a little sigh. "So here goes," I said. I wheeled my way down the hill and along the long walking trail to the start area. I'd spent so much time as host that I had to hurry now. Wally trotted along beside me with Amanda just behind him. When I finally made it to the start area, Wally pulled out my wet suit and handed it to me. I pulled it over the compression suit I wore (the compression suit helped hold in the muscles over which I lacked full control). Then I pulled on my swim cap and wheeled over closer to the start group.

Johnno and David Knight came over to me. "Let's do this," David said.

"Yep, let's do it," I said. I stood up from my chair. "I won't see you again for a while," I said as Wally took it away. I waded out into the water with just over one hundred other John Maclean Foundation competitors. Steve Waugh and Jock were there.

Craig Alexander, three-time Ironman world champion, came over and found me in the water. The two of us moved closer to the front of the group. "This is it," I said.

Craig smiled. "Glad I could share this day with you, mate."

"Me too," I said.

I looked over. The starter raised his hand. The buzzer sounded. We were off. The race had begun.

19

The Final Push

Daddy. Daddy. Open your eyes," I heard Jack say. To be honest, opening my eyes took more energy than I had at that point.

Before I lay down on the ground, I could see the finish line perhaps 100 or 150 meters ahead. I thought I had the strength to get there, but my body demanded I stop. I had to lie down. I could sense the crowd gathering around me. I felt the cold of ice under my neck. Someone poured water over my head. "Here, John, take a drink of Gatorade," someone said. I planned on having some as soon as I mustered up the strength to raise my head.

I never thought the heat would be the thing that would stop me so close to the end. Even though the calendar said midspring, the thermometer had other ideas. On the day I decided to walk two laps along a three-mile course around a lake with absolutely no protection from the sun, the temperature hovered near triple digits. To make matters worse, I had on a black compression suit under my clothes along with long black, legging-type socks stretched up the length of my legs. The socks protected my skin from the braces, but they also locked in my body heat.

"Daddy. Open your eyes," Jack pleaded. I planned to open them. I just needed a minute to rest first. *I wish we finished with the swim instead of starting with it*, I thought. *The cool lake would feel so nice right now.*

The lake had actually felt cold when I waded in five hours earlier. The water temperature hovered around seventy degrees, which was much warmer than the cold North Atlantic waters of the English Channel but still cool enough that almost all the competitors wore wet suits. Swimming a kilometer was, for me, refreshing. When I took a breath on my right side, I saw Craig Alexander, holding back to keep pace with me. One of the top triathletes in the world who specializes in 70.3 triathlons, also known as half Ironmans, Craig normally swims twice the distance we swam at the Nepean in roughly the same time we did on this day. But he wasn't out for time. He was there to share the day with me and the rest of our group.

When I took a breath on my left, I saw another Aussie legend, Ky Hurst. While the name may not ring a bell in the States, he is perhaps the greatest open-water distance swimmer Australia has ever produced. Swimming is huge Down Under, and he's one of the best. As I looked back and forth at these two champions, I had to smile and think, *How much better can it get?*

Just as I did on my practice run, I crawled on my hands and knees out of the water at the end of the swim leg. Amanda waited for me next to the chair the organizers had set out for me to use to put on my leg braces. The chair was the only special provision made for me, the only thing that set me apart from the rest of the thousand-plus athletes who came out of the water through the course of the day. Amanda handed me a towel and my socks. "How was the swim?" she asked.

"Incredible," I said. "The water felt great. What was my time?"

"A little over twenty-two minutes," Amanda replied.

"That's not too bad. Not too bad at all." I felt great. I pulled off my wet suit and put my cycling jersey on over my wet compression suit. I then pulled up my socks, attached the braces, put on my shoes, grabbed my walking poles, and headed off to the bike staging area. I had recently switched to a different brand of shoes than I had used in any of my training walks. The new shoes plus the modifications Darren made to my braces should, I thought, keep my feet from blistering as they did on both my 4K and 5K walks.

As I walked up the slight hill toward the staging area, the scene looked very different than it had the deserted Saturday afternoon of my practice run. Bikes and equipment covered the entire parking lot. Some of the bikes had already been returned by athletes who had completed the bike leg. A few of the starters from the first wave neared the finish line for the entire race by the time I came out of the water.

I walked through the barriers that kept spectators clear of the bikes. Most of the JMF bikes were concentrated on one end of the staging area. I smiled as I found my bike. "Even with taking extra time to put on my braces, I'm still out ahead of a lot of my wave!" I said to Amanda as I climbed on my bike.

Johnno, Ky, and Craig were waiting for me along with a few other friends. I strapped my right foot into the pedal, pushed off with my left, and said, "Let's go for a ride, guys." We quickly caught up with more of my friends. It took us a little over an hour to ride the eighteen miles. The race winner completed the bike leg in forty minutes. My time didn't bother me, nor did it bother any of the group riding with me. None of us were out to set any sort of personal bests. The bike leg truly was just a bunch of guys going out on their bikes for a fun Sunday-morning ride. To be honest, I don't think I stopped smiling the whole time. I didn't want the bike leg to end.

Unfortunately it did.

I knew my feet were in trouble before I had walked the length of two football fields. I recognized the discomfort of blisters forming from my experience on my two training walks. Walking from the bike staging area to the walking path around the main lake, I went down a slight hill. The walk leg then starts at the base of the bridge with the Olympic rings on it. I could feel every step. Amanda was right beside me, as she would be for the next three and a half hours. Initially, the group of walkers with me was relatively small. Much of the JMF triathlon group was just coming in from the bike leg and hadn't caught up with me yet. The walkers weren't scheduled to join me until my second lap around the lake.

With the discomfort building, I had to concentrate hard to keep moving, focusing on every step. *Right pole, left leg. Left pole, right leg*, over and over and over again. The sun was still climbing in the sky. The heat hadn't yet hit its peak. *Right pole, left leg. Left pole, right leg.* I could hear the people around me, even those watching as I went by. I overheard a young boy ask his father as I passed, "Who's that?"

"A legend," his dad replied.

I didn't feel much like a legend. *Right pole, left leg. Left pole, right leg.* A camera crew from *60 Minutes* and Channel 9 News rode in a golf cart in front of me, cameras rolling. Cell phones were raised all around as people recorded the moment. My fourteen-year-old niece, Alana, planted herself right next to me. She was keen to be a part of the action.

"How ya feeling, Johnny?" someone asked. I smiled and said something like good, or okay. I don't know exactly because the question was asked at least every two minutes by a different person throughout the entire walk.

We crossed the bridge and walked along the curved portion of the end of the lake. The main lake at the regatta center is nothing like the lakes you go out on for a day of fishing or waterskiing. Because it was designed for Olympic rowing and kayaking events, the lake is just under a mile and a half long and quite narrow. When I reached the side of the lake directly across from the regatta center grandstands, I noticed a soft patch of grass under a tree. "I need to stop for a moment to make an adjustment," I told Amanda. I lay down on my back as the growing parade of people around me came to a halt. The pain radiating up from my feet told me the blisters were growing, but I didn't dare take a look. Instead I adjusted my socks and the positioning of the brace under my foot, retied my shoes, took a drink of water, and was up and on my way.

The parade of walkers grew. Most of those who were supposed to join me on my second lap jumped in on the first. Conversations went on all around me. People seemed to be having a reasonably good time. Up from behind me I heard running footsteps. Jock and Steve shot past me. Jock called out, "See you at the finish line." He then broke out laughing as the two of them stopped and started walking alongside me.

"How are you doing, mate?" Steve asked.

"Good. You survived the swim?" I glanced over at Steve as I spoke, but only for a moment. What he and Jock didn't understand, what no one other than Amanda knew, was how much I had to concentrate to take each step. The effort I expended every time I lifted a foot and moved it out in front of me, physically and mentally, exceeded anything I had ever done before. Out in the middle of the English Channel, I could stroke through the water on autopilot. After so many practice miles, I could have swum in my sleep. The movement was automatic. Walking was not and is not still to this day an automatic movement for me. If I lose my concentration, I will fall down.

Right pole, left leg. Left pole, right leg. I kept moving on. We reached the curve on the upper end of the lake. About halfway around it I looked over at Amanda. "I need to rest for a moment," I said. We found a shady spot, and I sat down just long enough to drink more water. The sun was nearly directly overhead now. The temperature continued to climb. The pain level climbed as well. When I started out again, my gait was just a little slower than it had been before, but I don't think anyone really noticed. An almost party atmosphere started to develop in the growing crowd. Those who had completed the 10K as a run, not a walk, came back out on the course to join me. More people in JMF T-shirts came along as well. Johnno came up next to me and walked along with Amanda and me for a while. Wally was always just a step or two behind, lugging some of my gear for me.

As we neared the end of the first lap, the sound of the PA in the grandstands of the regatta center grew louder and louder. Matty Harris, the race MC, was giving out the awards for the finishers. The grandstands were nearly full. When I was perhaps two hundred yards out, I noticed Matty wasn't talking about finishers or their awards. "Here comes John Maclean, ladies and gentlemen," he said. "He spent twenty-five years in a wheelchair until he met Ken Ware and went through Ken's Ware K tremor therapy." The crowd began to applaud.

Fifty yards out, I heard Matty telling more of my story. People in the stands stood and looked my way. The closer I came, the more of my story he told. "He's back here, ladies and gentlemen, doing the race for which he was training when he was hit by an eight-ton truck on the M4." The crowd was now on its feet, cheering.

One hundred feet away from the grand stand, I noticed Matty wasn't up in the press box. I saw him up ahead in the middle of the path. He wasn't just telling my story. He was introducing me to the crowd, all of whom were cheering for me as if I were about to win the event. (I, in fact, finished in 986th position. My sister Marion even beat me, although I smoked her in the swim and bike legs.) When I was fully in front of the grandstands, Matty came over to me, microphone in hand, and interviewed me in front of the crowd, most of whom were there to support other people who ran the triathlon that day.

"How are you doing, John?" was Matty's first question. I gave the standard answer about how I felt. I went on to thank all the people who had come out to support us. Then I added, "I have one more lap and I hope to do you proud."

"It's been a long time, twenty-six years," Matty said. "Just tell us a little bit about what you've been up to."

"I've been learning to walk again," I replied. The crowd liked that answer. I went on to thank Ken Ware, who was nearby, and added some remarks about redefining what is possible for those in wheelchairs.

Matty then put his hand on my shoulder and said, "I just can't believe we're standing here having this conversation. You said you were going to do this and you are. You have five K to go. Look at all the people behind you. Thank you, John. We will see you when you get back." The crowd stood and cheered. "John Maclean! Everybody, John Maclean!" People walking with me got excited. A party broke out at the Nepean Triathlon! Everyone was having a great time.

But I had one more lap to go.

I pushed myself back up over the bridge. My gait had slowed even more. People kept talking to me, but I replied less and less. Amanda knew I was in great pain. I stopped for breaks a little more frequently. The party atmosphere was still in gear. Everyone around me was in high spirits. It looked like the scene from

Forrest Gump where he runs back and forth across the country. I love that movie, and on this day, I guess I was Forrest.

About halfway down the far side of the lake the pain in my feet finally became more than I could bear. Without announcing I was going to stop, I headed off the path. I lay down on my back and started untying my shoes. One of the guys following along jumped down on the ground right behind me so that I could use him as a pillow. The crowd gathered closer until a wall of people surrounded me. Johnno, David Knight, Steve, and Jock came in close. Amanda crouched down, right beside me. I pulled off my shoes and socks and braces to have a look at my feet. The soles looked like I had walked four and a half miles over sharp rocks. A few people gasped. The party was definitely over. It had been for me for a long time.

"I need some dry socks," I said. Wally dug around in my back-pack that he'd been carrying for me all day, but I hadn't thought to pack a second pair. David Knight sat down and pulled his socks off. "Here. You can have mine," he said.

But I needed more than socks. Darren, who had caught up to me not long before and had been walking quietly to the side observing me, came running up. He took my braces and started making adjustments. He pulled away part of the padding on the bottoms. "I don't know if it will make your feet feel any better now, but I think this will keep any new blisters from coming up," he said.

I pulled David's socks on, adjusted the braces, and pulled on my shoes. I lay there for just a moment longer. I seriously considered calling it quits, when Jock looked at me. "You've been lay-ing there long enough, John. Get up. What do you think this is, a bloody holiday? Get off your lazy bum and let's get going."

I needed guys like Jock around me.

Back on my feet, I still had a full half lap to go—a mile and a half, at least. I walked a short while before I needed to stop again. Before long I was back at it, but I needed to stop yet another time. The breaks came more and more frequently now. The temperature had hit triple digits. I started getting light-headed.

With a little over one kilometer to go, I had a surprise waiting for me: Jack. "Daddy!" he said, running up to me with a painted sign he'd made with Ashleigh. It said "Go Daddy Go." Just seeing him up close gave me an extra burst of energy. I sat down on a side rail and gave him a hug.

I walked a few more yards, when another special guest greeted me. A young boy with cerebral palsy named Aaryan joined me, pushing his walker. Using the walker is very difficult for Aaryan. He spends most of his time in his wheelchair. The two of us met during a previous foundation event, and we became fast friends. He calls me his hero, but the truth is, he's mine. Aaryan's family was with him. He was determined to come out and walk the last hundred meters with me.

A new energy came through the crowd once Jack and Aaryan joined our group. I could feel all my friends and supporters willing me to the finish line. The end wasn't much farther down the path. But the sun beat down and my head grew light. I sat down for a few minutes on a guardrail again next to the walking path. Amanda gave me some Gatorade and poured water over my head and back to try to cool me down. "I'm okay," I said. "Let's keep going."

When I was just over one hundred meters from the finish line, I suddenly knew I wasn't okay. The heat finally wore me down. "I need to lie down," I said. I closed my eyes, and everything just sort of went away.

"Daddy. Daddy. Open your eyes." Jack's voice came through

the fog that had overtaken me. "Daddy," he said. I mustered all the strength I had and sat up. Amanda handed me another Gatorade, which I downed.

"Are you okay, sweet? You're so close now," Amanda said.

"Let's finish this," I said.

I stood. The crowd applauded. I started moving toward the finish line. *Right pole, left leg. Left pole, right leg.* One step after another. Nothing I had ever done compared to the pain and exhaustion I now felt. Not the Ironman. Not the channel swim. And certainly not rowing. Nothing compared. The pain grew in intensity. Somewhere in the back of my mind I could hear Johnno's words from so long ago. *The pain won't last forever, but the memories will.* There was a memory I was determined to make, and nothing was going to stop me.

One hundred feet out from the finish line, I stopped one last time. "Would you carry these for me?" I asked David Knight as I handed him my walking poles. I turned to Amanda. "Ready?"

"Ready," she replied. We each held one of Jack's hands. Then the three of us walked the last one hundred feet and crossed the finish line. Together. Every challenge I had ever conquered, every Everest I had ever climbed, all built to this crescendo. Nothing I had ever done can compare, either in its degree of difficulty or in the pure joy I experienced. Amanda, Jack, and I crossed the line, not as the finish but as the beginning of a whole new world of possibilities. I cannot wait to see how far we now go, together.

20
Afterword

Every time I told my story, I was asked if I considered it to be a miracle. The only way I could truly answer that question was to take a look inside and see if that was indeed the case. For that, I had to have an MRI.

As strange as it seems now, the first MRI on my spine came twenty-six years after my accident. Although the technology was around in 1988, it was not yet widely available. Not that having it would have made a difference with any of the care I received. My medical team knew my spine was damaged quite severely. An MRI would have given them a visual image whereby they could see the full extent of that damage. Without that, they could only guess how many of the three million nerves that make up the spinal cord were still intact and how many were gone forever.

60 Minutes arranged for me to have my first MRI as part of the feature they did about me. They did so in part to try to find an explanation for exactly what had taken place as I had transitioned to walking again. People who spend twenty-five years in a wheelchair just don't get up and walk. The *60 Minutes* reporter, Georgie Gardner, interviewed the spinal specialist who has taken care of me since my accident, Dr. John Yeo, and asked what he thought had happened. A religious man, Dr. Yeo did not hesitate to call my recovery of function a miracle. The MRI was part of the search to see if that was truly the case. Dr. Yeo and I wanted to know: Had the nerves in my spinal cord regenerated themselves?

I stood in the back of the room as Dr. Yeo and radiologist Dr. David Brazier studied my scans on the screens in front of them. Dr. Brazier said, "You'll want to come on over here, John."

I walked over. Dr. Yeo stepped back to give me space. The room was quite small.

"You can see here," Dr. Brazier said, pointing a pen at what appeared to be a dark bubble along my spinal cord, "the lesion on your cord is clearly visible. Now take a look over here." He pointed to an image of a white, oblong shape that had a very small spot of dark just off-center on one side. "This is a cross section of the cord. The white area is the damaged cord, and this tiny bit over here"—he circled a small cluster of dark spots—"is the cord that remains. It is enough, in your case, obviously, for you to have some function. But to be honest with you, I am amazed seeing you walk forward just then, given the scans I have in front of me, because there is quite a lot of damage." To give you an idea of the ratio of healthy to dead nerves, if the image itself was a map of mainland America, the healthy nerves were about the size of Missouri.

I nodded and stared at the image on the screen. Finally seeing the actual injury, this leftover from my accident from so long ago, felt more than a little strange. Compared to the abrasions that covered my body, the lesion in my spinal cord was so small.

Dr. Yeo spoke up. "If we had done an MRI back in 1988, John, do you think it would look exactly the same as today?"

"Yes," I said. "I don't think it has changed at all. Many of the things I could not do in 1988, I still cannot do today."

"I believe you're right," said Dr. Yeo.

I did not need to go into detail for Dr. Yeo, but in brief, here are the things that had not changed: I'm still unable to lift my right foot up and down. I still lack the ability to move my legs away from the center of my body, which is called abduction. I still have very minimal flickers in my right glute, and I still have the same amount of tactile sensations in both legs that I had the day I woke up in the hospital with tubes running out of my body.

The MRI allowed me to see the enemy I'd been trying to beat for two and a half decades, but it still did not explain why I was now able to do things I had not been able to do for twenty-five years. How could I now walk? Three million nerves make up a healthy spinal cord. At my T12 vertebra, my working nerves number in the thousands, perhaps tens of thousands. Why did they suddenly allow me to walk? Am I a walking miracle? If I am not, does my ability to get up from my chair and leave my wheels behind offer hope and a road map for others with spinal cord injuries?

I wasn't the only one with these questions. The reporter from *60 Minutes* asked Dr. Yeo the same things as my MRI scans hung on light boards on the walls of the room. "Our interpretation of this is that it is not through regeneration that John is getting recovery of function but a resynapsing, an opening up of pathways." He later explained this to me. "Medically it appeared to me as miraculous. In analyzing your recent improvements, I believe this recent therapeutic approach could well have tapped into a method of loading messages into the spinal cord above, at, and possibly even below the injury, which have caused a cumulative effect. In the past a principle similar to this was well known to physical therapists as 'proprioceptive neuromuscular facilitation,' or PNF. This means remaining neural pathways 'wake up' rather than regenerate."

Essentially, what Dr. Yeo said was that the specific nerves that

carry the signal from my brain to my legs enabling me to walk survived the accident. However, the trauma of the accident and the
damage to the nerves around them caused these intact nerves to
switch off. Ken's therapy, then, in some way awakened these nerves
and caused them to begin to function once again. Similar results
have been observed since the 1930s and 1940s through PNF,
which was pioneered by a neurologist named Herman Kabat in
his work with children with cerebral palsy and other neurological
conditions. By tapping into the proprioceptive system, the sensory
processing system that has to do with our awareness of standing,
sitting, and so forth, Dr. Kabat was able to get his patients to move
in ways they had not before.* Dr. Yeo believes this is what happened to me.

If this is correct, could the same approach work with others
with spinal cord injuries? That's hard for me to say. I am an athlete, not a doctor. I can only speak of my experience. After my
accident, I retained functions below my injury, including sexual
function, as well as control of my bowels and urinary tract in addition to about 25 percent use of my left leg. That percentage has not
changed since my therapy with Ken began. I have not been cured
in the true sense of the word. I have regained function, in that I
can now walk again and spend prolonged periods of time out of
my chair with the use of my leg braces. If this can be explained
by my synapses awakening, then I suppose others might have the
same experience. Every spinal cord injury is unique. With three
million nerves to possibly damage, the odds that any two people
will damage the exact same combination are astronomical. That is

---

* Lee Burton and Heidi Brigham, "Proprioceptive Neuromuscular Facilitation:
The Foundation of Functional Training," FMS Screening, FMS, July 4, 2013,
http://www.functionalmovement.com/articles/Screening/2013-07-04_proprio-
ceptive_neuromuscular_facilitation_the_foundation_of_functional_training.

why it is so hard to predict how an injury in the exact same spot as mine, the T12, might affect a person.

Ken Ware offers a different explanation for why I can now walk. With a scientific background in physics, Ken approaches the body as a complex system that operates according to the basic laws of physics. Because he sees the body through this lens, he believes all of the body's systems and how they interact can be explained by these laws. Every system is interconnected, with each impacting the others. Ken includes every system, even the emotions. Practically speaking, this means that the responses in the body triggered by our emotions obey and can be explained by the basic laws of physics. The way this plays out in every person is often different and unpredictable. The key for him came when he discovered chaos theory. Chaos is used to study any sort of complex system where there is confusion and unpredictability. Other researchers use it to study things like the weather and the stock market. Ken uses it to study the body.

What does this mean for me? Ken's tremor therapy that enabled me to begin using my legs again grew out of his research. First he observed the tremors I described earlier in the book. Then he set out to understand them. What he found was that the body uses tremors to release a burst of energy that recalibrates the system. Trauma, physical and emotional, basically blocks the body's system from working properly, and pain is often the result. Repeated patterns emerge that reinforce the blocks, and chronic pain results. When my system recalibrated, my pain levels dropped dramatically. As my pain levels decreased, I was able to focus on the next part of Ken's research, the part that he uses to explain how and why I am walking.

When my spinal cord was injured, signals from my brain to my legs could no longer get through. If you think of the spinal cord as a highway, most of mine was blown up, and what was left was so crowded by the traffic of signals trying to squeeze into a small space that nothing could get through. This is an extreme oversimplification, but like I said, I am an athlete, not a doctor or a physicist. Through my twenty-five years of pursuing sports, I constantly and consistently stimulated the neurons—in effect, sending more and more signals down the blocked highway. The neurons, like people on a gridlocked interstate, did not like being backed up with nowhere to go. They sought out and finally found a way to get through.

Ken's explanation for my recovery of function, then, is that my body's neurological system adapted and found a way by sending signals through other nerves that run down my back outside of my spinal cord. Like blocked cars and trucks on a highway, they found an alternative route. The new paths were not enough in and of themselves. My entire neurological system needed to recalibrate to reset the hierarchy that acts like the traffic cop in the network. Before, neurons could not get through the new paths they created on other nerves because the body's system gave priority to whatever neurons originally used the road. With the reset, the signals I wanted to get through now got through.

Again, this is an oversimplification of how all this was explained to me. Ken has written extensively on this topic in research journals.

The way I see what has happened to me is, through Ken's work, I've been able to tap into the abilities that I have always had. Ken often said to me, "You were always able to do this; you just didn't have the right tools to unlock your system to allow alternative access." I do not believe I have experienced a miracle. To me, receiving the use of my legs is the end result of the journey on which I have traveled since immediately after my accident. If I had not constantly pushed myself to see how far I could go in my chair, always open to new challenges in different sports, then I would not be walking today. My ability to focus and challenge my mind and body to go on a journey of multiple sporting disciplines over the past twenty-seven years has assisted in my acceptance and embracing of this new research. On this both Ken and Dr. Yeo agree. I believe Ken has enabled me to tap into increased mobility by inducing managed tremors to recalibrate my system, and quieting the noise of my subconscious thought. On top of this, my life as a professional athlete gave me the freedom to devote hours upon hours every day to the exercise program Ken designed for me.

I don't think I have experienced a regeneration of my spinal cord up to this point. I don't know if I will in the future. I have no control over it either way, but we do now have an MRI that gives us a baseline against which to measure any future changes. This takes me back to my philosophy in all my endeavors in sports. I focus on controlling the controllables and not worrying about that which I cannot control.

And what I can control is setting my sights ahead, looking for the next challenge.

John Maclean invites you to contact and follow him at

www.johnmaclean.com.au

www.jmf.com.au

@johnmaclean27

johnmaclean.com.au

John Maclean logo by brand designer Hans Hulsbosch

Acknowledgments

There are many people to acknowledge for this book, but most of all the people who saved my life all those years ago and looked after me in Westmead and Royal North Shore hospitals. My family doctor, Dr. Atef Gabrael, and my spinal specialist Professor John Yeo, who guided me through my recuperation and back into the game of life.

I would like to thank my family, friends, business colleagues, and mentors who spent time revisiting my story with Mark Tabb in order to put this book together. Mark Tabb, thank you for your passion and enthusiasm for my story and the hours of research and writing, the many more hours of Skype calls late at night or early in the morning to accommodate our time differences and your commitment to making this a book we can both be proud of.

John Young and David Knight, I am so grateful for your friendship, support, and belief in me, always.

Ricky Jeffs, my friend and chairman of the John Maclean Foundation, Tiffany and the members of the board, our many supporters and sponsors—the work of the Foundation is enriched because of you.

To my agent Rachel Vogel, thank you for your direction and efforts on my behalf. You are a wonderful navigator.

To the team at Hachette Books, thank you for believing in my

Acknowledgments

There are many people to acknowledge for this book, but most of all the people who saved my life all those years ago and looked after me in Westmead and Royal North Shore hospitals. My family doctor, Dr. Atef Gabrael, and my spinal specialist Professor John Yeo, who guided me through my recuperation and back into the game of life.

I would like to thank my family, friends, business colleagues, and mentors who spent time revisiting my story with Mark Tabb in order to put this book together. Mark Tabb, thank you for your passion and enthusiasm for my story and the hours of research and writing, the many more hours of Skype calls late at night or early in the morning to accommodate our time differences and your commitment to making this a book we can both be proud of.

John Young and David Knight, I am so grateful for your friendship, support, and belief in me, always.

Ricky Jeffs, my friend and chairman of the John Maclean Foundation, Tiffany and the members of the board, our many supporters and sponsors—the work of the Foundation is enriched because of you.

To my agent Rachel Vogel, thank you for your direction and efforts on my behalf. You are a wonderful navigator.

To the team at Hachette Books, thank you for believing in my story, for your patience and guidance, and for ensuring this book has the best possible care as it finds its way to readers.

Ken and Nickie Ware, you are extraordinary humans. You saw the possibilities and gave me no limits, and I'm forever grateful to you for bringing my life full circle and giving me the tools and the confidence to close one door and open another, behind which was a world of new challenges and possibilities. Possibilities I always dreamed of.

To Darren Pereira, thank you for taking the time to contact me and for introducing me to NeuroMuscular Orthotics. It is your ongoing support of me (and my legs) which is allowing me to truly see how far I can go.

To my beautiful wife, Amanda, you're always beside me, encouraging me to chase my dreams. Thank you—for everything.

Finally to my son, Jack, my greatest achievement. You are the light I look to when things get tough, the love that motivates and drives me, and the reality check when all you need from me is to play dinosaurs.